the outdoor
DUTCH OVEN
cookbook

the *outdoor* DUTCH OVEN *cookbook*

SECOND EDITION

SHEILA MILLS

New York Chicago San Francisco Lisbon London Madrid Mexico City
Milan New Delhi San Juan Seoul Singapore Sydney Toronto

The McGraw·Hill Companies

Library of Congress Cataloging-in-Publication Data

Mills, Sheila.
    The outdoor Dutch oven cookbook / Sheila Mills. — 2nd ed.
        p.   cm.
    ISBN 0-07-154659-6
    1. Dutch oven cookery.   2. Outdoor cookery.   I. Title.

  TX840.D88M55   2008
  641.5'89—dc22   2008031655

3 4 5 6 7 8 9 10 11 12 13 14 15 16 DOC/DOC 1 9 8 7 6 5 4 3 2 1

ISBN 978-0-07-154659-1
MHID   0-07-154659-6

Illustration on page 7 by Ruth Osterhout; illustration on page 9 by Dan Kirchoff; all other illustrations by Parry Merkley

McGraw-Hill books are available at special quantity discounts to use as premiums and sales promotions or for use in corporate training programs. To contact a representative, please e-mail us at bulksales@mcgraw-hill.com.

Contents

Foreword

Taking duffle bags and wet suits in hand, we left black-top lights and auto horns behind and entered a new river and mountain experience. Two Church sons, five grandchildren, and a daughter-in-law and her parents joined the launch onto Idaho's Middle Fork of the Salmon River in the Frank Church River of No Return Wilderness, named for my husband, Frank. We joined with strong young river guides on an unparalleled wilderness float.

Dave and Sheila Mills of Rocky Mountain River Tours run a superb trip, which is topped only by the magical cliffs, the pristine tumbling river, and the unmatched dining provided by Sheila's Dutch oven dinners, served each evening after fun-filled days. The Dutch oven dining was the frosting on the cake—and it often was a Dutch oven cake.

Somehow eating like this by the campfire, with night falling on the roaring river, adds to the ambiance of a truly glorious mountain river trip.

Taking home Sheila's recipes makes a year-long reminder of a time away from the din and the rush of everyday life. We all recommend the Rocky Mountain River Tours—and Sheila's Dutch oven recipes—to add to a memorable experience.

Bethine Church
Boise, Idaho

Acknowledgments

A big thank you to all my friends who contributed their favorite recipes. A special thanks to those of you who shared with David and me the results of recipe testing.

To Harrison Hilbert for updating the section on camp standards and kitchen ethics, whether in your backyard or on a river bank in the wilderness. Once again a thank you to good friends, Jerry Myers for his "Catch-and-Release Fishing" section and Ruth Osterhout for the dishwater-strainer sketch.

Rocky Mountain River Tours' rafting guides deserve hugs all around for preparing my recipes in fine style with delicious results for sixteen weeks straight during our rafting season. Keep in mind that the guides are cooking three meals a day for twenty-four customers and friends over six days. Idaho's "world famous" Middle Fork of the Salmon runs 100 miles through the heart of the Frank Church River of No Return Wilderness, the largest roadless/motorless wilderness in the continental United States.

What an honor having Bethine Church write the Foreward. She is an Idaho icon and good friend.

I could not have done any of this without the loving guidance and gentle pushing of my best friend and mate, David. He is my best critic and cheerleader.

I hope you enjoy *The Outdoor Dutch Oven Cookbook* created as a result of recipe requests from thirty years of repeat river trip guests.

Introduction

All of the recipes in this book are geared to cooking outdoors. They can, however, be easily adapted to indoor cooking. The recipes have been tested at home in a conventional kitchen as well as outdoors in a Dutch oven. The Dutch oven is an ancient cooking tool, and I hope you will help to keep it alive for many years to come.

David, my husband, and I operate Rocky Mountain River Tours, an outfitting business on the Middle Fork of the Salmon River in Idaho's Frank Church River of No Return Wilderness. We are fortunate to be able to share this beautiful country with people from all over the world, who come to float the river with us and our crew for a week's vacation. Part of this unforgettable experience for our guests is observing the creation of and dining on the

exceptional meals prepared in Dutch ovens in a Rocky Mountain outdoor setting.

I think most people like to try something new. Buy a Dutch oven, try these recipes, and then adapt them to create your own meals. I hope you will enjoy the results and that this book will prove exciting and helpful.

If you are interested in experiencing truly excellent Dutch oven cooking in one of the most pristine wilderness environments in the world, you are invited to write to Rocky Mountain River Tours for a brochure on excursions on the Middle Fork of the Salmon River in Idaho.

Write or call Rocky Mountain River Tours, P.O. Box 8596, Boise, ID, 83707, (208) 345-2400, or visit rockymountainrivertours.com.

Dutch Oven Care and Use

The Dutch oven is a versatile cooking pot that substitutes for a host of outdoor cooking utensils. With its snug-fitting lid in place, it becomes an oven when heated with charcoal briquettes. Food can be baked, braised, stewed, or roasted. With the lid removed, the oven becomes a kettle for boiling, deep-fat frying, or heating food quickly over a fire. Even the lid doubles in service—it can be converted into a frying pan.

A true camp Dutch oven is easily identified by its legs, which extend below the oven and permit it to sit over hot coals, and its flat lid, which has a vertical lip around the outside edge to retain the hot coals that are placed on top.

There are several types of Dutch ovens on the market. The camp Dutch oven is not regularly stocked by supermarkets and hardware stores, so you may need to order it directly from the manufacturer or a river supply or outdoor equipment catalog. The important thing to watch for when purchasing a Dutch oven for outdoor use is that it is not simply a flat-bottomed kettle made for kitchen cooking. If you plan to prepare the recipes at home using a conventional oven and stove, a flat-bottomed Dutch oven will suffice.

The camp Dutch oven is made specifically for outdoor cooking. It is made of heavy cast-iron or aluminum, and comes in basic sizes from 8 to 24 inches in diameter, and from 4 to 6 inches deep.

The cast-iron Dutch oven is heavy, thick, and flat on the bottom, with three short legs. The lid is tight-fitting and has a vertical lip with a handle in the center. There also is a bail for lifting the entire unit. Proper seasoning of a cast-iron camp Dutch oven is essential. If you scour your oven with strong detergents, it will need reseasoning frequently. Rub the oven with unsalted shortening, place it in a 400°F oven until it smokes, and then wipe out the excess fat. If you are camping, just place it on the coals with the lid on until it smokes. Then wipe it out. If you wash it with detergent between uses, it is a good idea to oil it to keep it from rusting. It is best, too, to store a cast-iron Dutch oven upside down and with the lid off.

The aluminum Dutch oven is popular with campers because it is lightweight, rustproof, and requires no seasoning. However, cast iron, though it is heavier than aluminum and takes longer to heat, heats evenly and stays hot for a long period of time. It is important that you do not overheat an aluminum oven, because you can damage it permanently. The aluminum Dutch oven is one-third the weight of the cast iron, and thus it is more portable on camping trips. It is the only model that can be backpacked by a hiker. The two types cost about the same.

Use charcoal briquettes to heat your Dutch oven, allowing twenty to thirty minutes for them to heat properly before placing them around the oven. It is a good idea to preheat the lid when baking, to prevent heat from being drawn out of the porous iron by cold ingredients.

Most of the following recipes are adapted for six to eight servings and can be prepared in a 10- or 12-inch oven. An aluminum oven heats quickly and requires five to eight briquettes evenly distributed underneath and twelve to sixteen briquettes on the lid for a 12-inch oven. Using additional coals to try to speed up the cooking time is unwise, since it can damage the aluminum and cause the food to burn.

Cast iron requires more cooking time than aluminum, but the number of coals on top and bottom remains the same. Either the cast-iron or aluminum Dutch oven can be permanently damaged by pouring cold water into a hot oven, by uneven heating caused by putting coals on only half the oven or lid, by careless packing while traveling (the legs can be broken off or pushed up through the bottom by too much jamming), and by rust and corrosion.

The lid, turned upside down on the coals, can be used for frying. When using more than one oven, the second can be stacked on top of the first, and so on.

When checking for doneness, do not leave the lid off any longer than necessary. It is equivalent to opening your oven door at home—you will lose all the heat. It is very important that the lid remain tightly sealed.

The original camp Dutch oven evolved through centuries of experience. It was designed for cooking complete meals on open fires without the need for other appliances (a shovel, pliers, and leather gloves come in handy, though). It is at once a kettle, a frying pan, an oven, a pot, and a stove—all in one portable utensil.

A unique cooking device, the Dutch oven can produce delicious and nutritious meals with little trouble or skill. To demonstrate the talents of the camp Dutch oven, I have included recipes for a variety of dishes in this cookbook. If you are not acquainted with an authentic camp Dutch oven, I suggest you make friends with one right away. Use your oven to prepare leisurely campsite meals, and then settle back and enjoy some of the most delectable dishes you have ever eaten.

Temperature Control

Different foods and dishes require different cooking temperatures. The following guide is for an aluminum Dutch oven. Increase the number of briquettes by about one-fourth for a cast-iron oven. Actual temperatures will vary because of charcoal quality and weather.

When coals are hot they are barely covered with white ash, and you can hold your hand near them for only a few seconds. The objective is to get the oven hot enough to cook the food before it dries out, yet not so hot you can't control the cooking process. In most cases, if the food is sputtering and popping a lot, the heat is too high. Using the tongs, remove about one fourth of the briquettes at a time from the top and underneath until the cooking subsides.

Desired Temperature Range (degrees F)	Number of Briquettes for 10"-Oven	Number of Briquettes for 12"-Oven
250–300—Low	8 on top, 4 under	12 on top, 6 under
300–350—Medium	10 on top, 4 under	15 on top, 6 under
350–400—Hot	12 on top, 5 under	18 on top, 8 under

The Cooking Environment

A few simple rules of conduct can help contribute to low-impact cooking in camp and the perpetuation of beautiful, natural campsite environments. Things to consider for low-impact cooking include the following:

Gas Stoves

Use whenever possible, especially in areas where fire danger is high, where driftwood is scarce (e.g., on desert rivers or during drought years), and anytime on popular, high-use rivers.

Efficient propane stoves are favored by many boaters.

A 2½-gallon propane cylinder provides adequate fuel for a party of fifteen for a six-day trip, with the stove used for about half of the cooking tasks and the remainder done with charcoal on a grill or in Dutch ovens (this does not include heating wash water on the stove).

Charcoal Briquettes

Briquettes provide consistent, long-lasting heat.

The impact of wood-gathering around campsites decreases.

Ash residue is minimized.

A 10-pound bag of briquettes will provide cooking heat for six Dutch ovens, which will serve thirty people.

Firepans and Ashes

A firepan can be made from sheet metal with 3- to 4-inch sides to contain ashes.

Steel oil drain pans, which are available from auto parts stores, make excellent firepans for small groups. The round pans have 3- to 4-inch sides, nest together, and are a perfect size for a Dutch oven.

Firepans eliminate proliferation of unsightly fire rings and reduce the demand for wood, because users tend to build smaller fires.

Use of a firepan helps prevent wildfires.

Firepans are required on many rivers.

Firepans prevent the spread of ash or charcoal on beaches and in camps.

Elevate your firepan on rocks, if possible, to protect the soil and surrounding vegetation. If you are not able to elevate it, put it on bare sand or a gravel bar, where it will do the least damage to soil organisms.

Trash Disposal

Each morning before breaking camp, some groups turn their cookfire into a refuse incinerator. Burning garbage, especially plastics, in the cookfire produces objectionable smoke and fumes. I recommend packing your plastic, aluminum, and paper products and food scraps for recycling or disposal at a designated landfill.

Manage your campfire to produce the least amount of residue.

After your fire has burned completely down, stir into the embers a small amount of water, unused coffee, or dishwater.

Transfer mixture into an airtight surplus 20-mm ammo can or a similar metal or plastic container. Bring enough cans to contain such residue for your group for the entire trip, and transfer to an official landfill when you return.

At your next campsite, recycle the ash to cover the bottom of your firepan, which will reduce the ash further and eliminate warping of the pan.

Do not dump residue into rivers or streams, because it will be deposited back onto the beaches and banks.

The environmental impact along streams and river corridors is significantly reduced by the use of firepans and low-impact camping.

Etiquette for Gathering and Burning Firewood

Never cut or burn live vegetation.

Use downed or dead wood that you can break by hand for fuel. Standing dead wood is part of the natural setting and provides a natural habitat for birds and small animals.

Do not bring hazardous, thorny, or sharp pieces of wood into the camp area for use as fuel.

Never collect firewood that is thicker than your forearm.

Keep your fire as small as possible.

Designate an area to break wood for fire fuel, and make sure this area is left looking natural before departing camp.

RUTH OSTERHOUT

Making a dishwater strainer.

Your firepan should be located in a level, safe area, where the flames or heat will not ignite overhead branches or nearby objects.

You might want to designate a member of your group to be responsible for a safe, efficient campfire.

Gloves, pliers, a shovel, and shoes are essential for your protection and convenience in working with the fire and charcoal.

Do not build your campfire bigger than necessary.

There is generally no need for an ax or saw for firewood preparation.

Disposal of Waste Water

Never pour unused juices or fluids on the ground or in a stream, as they may attract flies, yellowjackets, chipmunks, and bears. Pour them into your garbage container (an airtight, 20-mm ammo can) if camping on a river. Some of the fluid can also be poured into the lower edge of your firepan, where it will boil off.

Never pour waste water or fluids into an outhouse, because it retards biodegradation. Fecal material in a pit privy must be dry to reach the necessary 140°F temperature in order to biodegrade.

Strain dishwater above the high-water level and far away from camp. Put solid particles in your trash container. Fabric paint strainers work well. They are available at hardware stores.

A strainer can be made with a piece of window screen stretched over a ring cut from a 5-gallon plastic bucket. Cut two rings from a tapered bucket, which will interlock around the screen when pushed together. Secure with pop rivets (see illustration).

Strain the first wash bucket first and use the last rinse to wash down the others.

Drinking Water

To prevent contamination of food and water when camping, personal and environmental cleanliness are vitally important. All backcountry water should be considered potentially contaminated by cryptosporidia, giardia, or bacteria that can cause a variety of diseases. When carrying water is not practical, you will have to kill or remove the disease-causing organisms by heat, chemical, or mechanical disinfection of the water. To treat water use the following steps:

1. Filter the water to remove as many solids as possible.
2. Bring it to a rolling boil, and boil for a full minute.
3. Let it cool at least 30 minutes.
4. Add 8 drops of liquid chlorine bleach per gallon of cool water. Water must be cool or chlorine will dissipate and be rendered useless.
5. Let the water stand 30 minutes.
6. If it smells of chlorine, you can use it. If it does not smell of chlorine, add 8 more drops of bleach and let it stand another 30 minutes. Smell it again. You can use it if it smells of chlorine. You can also test it with chlorine litmus papers available at any spa supply store.
7. The only accepted measurement of chlorine (or water treatment agents) is the drop. A drop is specifically measurable. Use a dropper purchased at the drugstore. Other measures such as "capful" or "scant teaspoon" should not be used.

In addition to common household bleach, several other types of chemical treatment are available, such as iodine tablets, iodide crystals, and halazone tablets. Some people have allergic reactions to iodine products. Follow the instructions on the package for proper use.

After adding a chemical treatment to cold water, you must lengthen the contact (sitting) time to destroy cryptosporidia and giardia that might be present. Very cold water may take as long as four times the normal contact time.

Along wilderness rivers, where human contamination is minimal, a water filter featuring a cleanable ceramic cartridge is ideal for preparing water for drinking and food preparation. These filters are available at most river supply companies and some sporting goods and camp stores. For large groups of people for extended trips, the Water Purifier from Partner Steel is very good. Other filters are offered by Katadyn, PUR, MSR, First Need, and Sweet Water. A gravity-fed filter is available in which you fill a bag with water, hang it over a branch, and have it drip through the filter element into a bucket. It is not very fast, but it works well and doesn't require much effort.

You will need containers in which to store your water during the day. If there is a large group, you might want four 5-gallon cooler/dispensers. From them, people can fill their individual water bottles. If you are rafting, make sure everyone has a full water bottle, and that you have a 1- or 2-gallon container full on each raft for resupply. Each person should have a minimum of 2 liters of water each day. Remember to disinfect the water containers with chlorine bleach on a regular basis.

A handwash bucket.

DAN KIRCHOFF

Camp/River Sanitation

The only acceptable way to carry garbage is in an airtight metal or plastic container. Carrying garbage in a plastic bag alone is inadequate because the bags tear easily and are impossible to secure to a boat to prevent loss in case of an accident.

Have a 5-gallon handwash bucket available at all meals for the cooks and everyone who is sharing the food. For each handwash bucket, use an 8-ounce plastic measuring cup with an open handle to hang on the side of the bucket, with a small hole drilled in the bottom to dispense the water. Add 1½ to 2 tablespoons of bleach per 5-gallon bucket of water, as mentioned above. To wash hands, fill the measuring cup with bleach water and hang it by the handle over the edge of the bucket; wash hands as water flows from the hole in the bottom of the cup. Do not use this handwash bucket to wash food.

An improvement over a simple bucket is the Wishy-Washy hand-washing station from Partner Steel. Made of stainless steel, it clamps onto the side of a bucket of regular river water. You just step on the pump to get the flow going and it filters out the large sediment, leaving you clean water to wash your hands.

No one with the symptoms of a communicable disease, especially diarrhea, should be allowed to prepare food or handle utensils for other people.

Insist that everyone wash their hands with soap and water after using the toilet. Follow the same disinfecting procedure for the handwash bucket, as stated above.

Scrape food residue with a rubber spatula from plates and Dutch ovens into your garbage container. This helps keep dishwater cleaner.

To wash dishes, use buckets that can be heated on the fire or stove. (Use three buckets of water heated to boiling, with 1½ to 2 tablespoons of bleach per 5-gallon bucket for sanitizing.)

Wash Dutch ovens and cooking pots last to avoid fouling the wash and rinse water.

The final rinse temperature should be too hot to immerse your hands in the water.

Nondisposable plates are very handy on camping trips and do not create garbage the way paper ones do. Use plates at all meals to prevent food droppings. No food or watermelon seeds should be left on the ground to attract insects and small animals. Remember that popular campsites are occupied every night and can be impacted by careless camp practices.

Use only knives from the kitchen kit for food preparation. These should be washed after each meal. Personal knives should not be used in food preparation, especially folding knives, which harbor bacteria.

Separate your glass and aluminum bottles and cans from the rest of your trash. These can be recycled in most cities.

Human Waste Disposal

Because of the impact on soils, vegetation, and hazards associated with burial of feces, on some rivers human wastes should be packed into a portable toilet for disposal at a sanitary landfill or RV dump station. This type of "pack it out" policy for fecal material is a requirement for boaters on wild and scenic rivers. A procedure that has proved effective on such rivers is to use a 20-mm airtight ammo can fitted with a toilet seat. Plastic seats molded especially to fit on ammo cans are available in fashion colors from river equipment suppliers. Use a deodorant chemical. Have a water dispenser and soap available for handwashing.

In remote locations where toilets are unavailable and "pack it out" practices for human waste are not needed, feces should be disposed of in a place where they will not pollute water and will not be found by others. The recommended policy currently emphasizes burial of human feces in small latrines ("catholes") located at least 300 feet from the nearest surface water. Group use of single latrines at overnight campsites is not generally recommended since such concentration of human waste tends to increase the health hazard.

One-quart sealable plastic bags can be given to each person on the trip as a "container" for microtrash (tampons, tissue, toilet paper, and so forth). Each camper can fill his or her bag, put it with the group garbage, and get a new bag as needed.

Practice No-Kill, Catch-and-Release Fishing
by Jerry Myers

Trout fishing is becoming one of America's fastest-growing outdoor sports and an important activity of many river users. Unfortunately, our trout streams, and the trout populations sustained by these streams, are finite. Many streams contain unique subspecies of trout that do not exist elsewhere. Killing wild trout, regardless of local regulations, is not a viable option if we want to ensure quality fishing in years to come. We do not have to give up fishing, nor do we have to witness a decline in the fishing quality of our favorite streams. We do, however, have to practice proper, no-kill, catch-and-release fishing methods. Regardless of how carefully we catch and release trout, a certain number will die. The following tips will help keep fish mortality to a minimum:

Use a single barbless hook of the proper size. If your hooks are barbed, simply pinch the barb down flat with needlenose pliers or fishing forceps. Break or cut off two hooks on lures with treble hooks and pinch the barb on the remaining hook. Hooks that are too large for the fish you are catching can pierce the brain or the eyes of the fish.

Limit the time you play the fish. A hooked fish builds lactic acid in its tissues that can cause shock and even death. Excessively light tackle extends landing time and can overstress the fish. Use adequate tackle.

Limit your handling of the fish. Use fishing forceps or a hook disgorger to remove the hook, and leave the fish in the water, if possible. Do not squeeze the fish or handle it by the gills or gill covers. Never pick up a trout by its gills or by its lower jaw. If you must handle a fish, do it over the water, not in a boat or over the shore. If you cannot handle a fish in or over the water, you are in the wrong position. Change it.

If the hook is in the fish's throat or is difficult to remove, cut the line as close to the hook as possible and release the fish. The hook will rust out quickly. If you must use a net, leave the netted fish in the water. Choose a net of soft cotton or nylon netting.

Exhausted fish should be gently held in swimming position underwater until the fish is able to swim away under its own power. A gentle back-and-forth movement will help it breathe, or hold it so that it is facing upstream in the current.

If you want a photograph of the fish, make sure it is revived, and leave it in the water until your camera is ready. Gently grasp the fish just in front of the tail fin and support the fish's body by placing your other hand under its belly. Lifting larger fish requires having more support when lifting. Never grab for the fish if it slips from your hands, and always handle the fish over the water. You can get beautiful photographs and still leave the fish in the water by simply turning the fish onto its side on the surface of the water. Never drop or throw a fish back into the water.

Remember that every fish you hook is at risk. Trying to catch as many fish as you can, as fast as you can, will result in higher mortality rates. Take time to enjoy the many other aspects of fishing. You may want to fish with a hookless fly or lure. Often the greatest satisfaction is getting a fish to take a fly or lure, not necessarily setting the hook. Teach others the importance of wild fish and proper, no-kill, catch-and-release practices.

Jerry Myers, of Salmon, Idaho, is a fishing and river outfitter on the Wild Salmon River and is one of Idaho's top authorities on fishing.

Keeping Food Cold and Fresh

Ice chest performance is affected by numerous factors, including air temperature, cooler insulating capacity, the ratio of food to ice, and the frequency and conditions under which the chest is opened. Compared to small coolers,

large ice chests generally are better insulated and have more favorable surface-to-volume ratios, which means they will keep food colder longer using the same amount of ice as smaller coolers.

Unless special precautions are taken (such as supplementing water ice with a block of dry ice in a "deep freeze" meat cooler), midsummer boaters can expect that their ice supplies will be exhausted after about a week under ideal operation. That time can be cut in half if the cooler is operated poorly.

An approach to ice chest management favored by some boaters is to dedicate one or more coolers for the second half of their first week. For example, all perishable foods for days four through six might be packed in one chest and taped shut. In addition to extending the chilling capacity by cutting down on cooler opening, this approach can save time searching for food items during the first half of the trip. River scientist J. T. Brock has collected data on cooler performance under outfitted river trip conditions. In these studies, a 151-quart Igloo ice chest was wired with probes and a portable computer that recorded air, water, and internal cooler temperatures at the bottom, middle, and top of the chest. The study documented the presence of substantial temperature gradients within the ice chests. Four days into a July trip on the Middle Fork of the Salmon River, with maximum air temperatures in the low 90s, while block ice was chilling the bottom of the cooler to 34°F, the temperature at the top of the cooler approached 70°F. This thermal stratification should be borne in mind when positioning foods in an ice chest; place especially perishable or heat-sensitive items close to the ice at the bottom of the chest.

Block ice aged at sub-zero temperatures is preferable because of ice density.

To avoid unnecessary opening, label each cooler, using a felt-tip marker, which can be washed off at the end of the trip.

The Complete Camp and River Kitchen

Firepan

Cooking grate with adjustable legs (to fit inside firepan)

Dutch ovens, saucepans, and skillets, as needed for the menu

Pancake griddle

Water filter (if not cleanable, take along a spare cartridge)

Galvanized metal buckets for dishwashing

Handwash buckets (plastic) with dispensing plastic measuring cups, or handwashing pump

Partner Steel Wishy Washy Soap for washing dishes and hands

Chlorine bleach

Coffeepot(s)

Shovel

Gas stove (preferably propane or white gas)

Spice kit

Screened dishwater strainer

Cups (reusable), with storage bag

Plates (reusable), with storage bag

Eating utensils (metal), with storage bag

Portable table with oilcloth or vinyl tablecloth

Cutting boards (absorbent wood should not be used)

Mixing bowls

Culinary knives with blade guards

Hard plastic and rubber spatulas

Cooking utensils (as needed for your menu)

Sponges and scrubbers

Compartmentalized canvas roll-up bag for utensils

Wooden matches in waterproof container or butane fire igniter

Charcoal briquettes and lighter fluid

Corkscrew, can opener, and bottle opener

Thermos or airpot for coffee, tea, and/or hot water

Cloth dishtowels

Work gloves

Time-Saving Tips

When baking breads and cakes, line your Dutch oven with parchment or baker's paper to prevent sticking. Cut the paper into rounds to fit your Dutch oven. Parchment is available at any bakery. When the recipe calls for a pastry dough, you can use a commercially packaged crust, such as Krusteaz pie crust mix, my favorite.

To save on knife blades and on time, purchase canned foods that are already chopped, such as black olives and green chiles.

Wash produce prior to your trip. Spin-dry the lettuce and leafy green vegetables and put them in a zip-top bag with a paper towel. They will keep for a week in a cooler.

Premeasure and mix the dry ingredients for cakes and breads and put them in labeled zip-top bags prior to your trip.

Prepare salad dressings, dips, and sauces in advance and put them in sealed containers.

If you are going to serve a pasta salad, make it ahead of time if it is to be used in a day or two. If it won't be served until later in the trip, you can still cook the pasta in advance.

Slice, grate, and chop food items in advance to take advantage of your food processor at home and save time on your trip. You also have less waste to deal with on the trail.

Portion out meat and other items, heat-seal them in plastic bags, and freeze them in advance of your trip.

It helps to make a menu listing the items used so that all the people involved in your trip can assist in meal preparation.

Pack items into your cooler(s) according to when they will be used. Mark coolers and other storage containers as to their contents.

Use a wine bottle to roll out dough.

Carry utensils in a sealed, plastic container and take several hand towels to avoid using paper towels.

Resources for "The Cooking Environment":
Meyer, Kathleen. How to Shit in the Woods: An Environmentally Sound Approach to a Lost Art. *Ten Speed Press: Berkeley, California, 1989.*
Cole, David N. Low-Impact Recreational Practices for Wilderness and Backcountry. *U.S. Department of Agriculture Forest Service Intermountain Research Station, Ogden, Utah. General Technical Report INT-265, 1989.*
"Leave No Trace Outdoor Skills," www.lnt.org.

Breakfast Dishes

Remember

When a recipe calls for baking, braising, stewing, or roasting, the Dutch oven must be covered with charcoal briquettes on top of the lid. For boiling, frying, sautéing, and quick heating, leave the Dutch oven cover off. For more on cooking techniques for the Dutch oven, see "Dutch Oven Care and Use," pages 2–4. When using a conventional oven, preheat the oven to the given baking temperature.

SKOOKUMCHUCK SCRAMBLED EGGS

⅓ cup minced scallions
¼ green bell pepper, seeded and minced
2 tablespoons unsalted butter
24 eggs, well beaten
¼ cup bacon bits
2 tablespoons dried parsley flakes
¼ cup milk
8 ounces cheddar cheese, grated (2 cups)

These eggs are named for a creek flowing into the Salmon River. Skookumchuck means "strong rapid."

Sauté scallions and green pepper in butter in Dutch oven until tender. Add beaten eggs, bacon bits, and parsley, and mix well. Stir frequently until eggs are cooked. Add milk and cheese and stir until cheese melts. Serve immediately.

Yield: 10 to 12 servings

BREAKFAST FONDUE

butter for greasing pan
6 slices whole wheat bread, cubed
6 ounces cheddar cheese, grated
    (1½ cups)
⅓ pound link sausage (can use bulk)
3 eggs
2 cups milk
½ teaspoon dry mustard
1 10½-ounce can cream of mushroom soup

This delicious breakfast dish recipe was given to me by my aunt, Mac Oliver, from Billings, Montana, where she serves it every year for Christmas brunch. If you are not camping, begin this recipe the night before you are to serve it. However, it can also be prepared to be served immediately.

Butter a large casserole dish or Dutch oven. Place bread cubes in dish. Sprinkle with cheese. Brown the sausage, then drain and cut into thirds (or crumble if using bulk sausage). Place over cheese.

In a separate bowl, beat eggs slightly with 1⅔ cups milk and dry mustard. Pour egg mixture over sausage. Refrigerate overnight, unless you are camping.

Dilute soup with ⅓ cup milk and pour over all. Bake in Dutch oven for about 1 hour. For conventional oven, bake at 300°F for 1½ hours or until set.

Yield: 6 to 8 servings

EGGS BENEDICT

8 eggs
4 English muffins
8 thin slices ham, broiled or Canadian
    bacon
Jiffy Hollandaise sauce (see recipe on
    page 84) or 1 package dry instant
    hollandaise sauce
1 teaspoon paprika

Poach eggs. (If using a Dutch oven, fill half full with water and bring to a boil. Remove from heat. Add eggs to water and replace lid on Dutch oven for 3 to 5 minutes.)

Split and toast the English muffins. Top each half with a thin slice of broiled ham or Canadian bacon. Place a poached egg on the ham.

Prepare hollandaise sauce and pour over all. Sprinkle with paprika and serve immediately.

Yield: 8 servings

FANCY EGG SCRAMBLE

Cheese Sauce
2 tablespoons unsalted butter
2 tablespoons unbleached all-purpose flour
½ teaspoon salt
⅛ teaspoon black pepper
2 cups milk
4 ounces cheddar cheese, grated (1 cup)

Egg Scramble
1 cup diced Canadian bacon
⅓ cup chopped scallions
¼ pound fresh mushrooms, sliced
3 tablespoons unsalted butter
12 eggs, well beaten
4 teaspoons unsalted butter, melted
2¼ cups bread crumbs (or 3 slices bread,
    grated)
⅛ teaspoon paprika

Make the cheese sauce: Melt butter in a saucepan. Blend in flour, salt, and pepper. Add milk. Cook, stirring all the while, until bubbly. Stir in cheddar cheese and cook until melted. Set aside.

Make the egg scramble: In Dutch oven or skillet, cook Canadian bacon, scallions, and mushrooms in butter until onion is tender but not brown. Add eggs and scramble until just set.

Fold eggs into cheese sauce. Pour into Dutch oven or 9″ × 11″ casserole dish.

In a separate bowl, combine the melted butter, crumbs, and paprika; sprinkle over eggs.

Cover Dutch oven and bake for 15 minutes; remove top coals and bake slowly from bottom another 10 minutes. For conventional oven, bake at 375°F for 15 minutes.

Yield: 8 to 10 servings

AVOCADO FRITTATA

1 tablespoon unsalted butter
2 tablespoons olive oil
1 small onion, chopped
1 garlic clove, minced
½ teaspoon salt
freshly ground black pepper to taste
½ teaspoon dried basil
½ teaspoon dried oregano
6 eggs, well beaten
2 avocados, sliced
4 ounces cheddar cheese, grated (1 cup)
salsa for topping

Heat butter and olive oil in 10" Dutch oven or ovenproof skillet over medium heat. Sauté onion and garlic. Add salt, pepper, basil, and oregano.

Increase heat to high and pour in eggs, letting the uncooked egg flow under vegetables as you would for an omelet. Reduce the heat to medium. Top with avocados and cheese.

Cover pan. For Dutch oven, use coals on top and underneath and bake for 10 minutes or until the frittata is firm. For conventional oven, bake at 400°F for 10 minutes or until firm. Cut in wedges to serve. Top with salsa.

Yield: 6 servings

BROKEN OAR BREAKFAST BURRITOS

12 ounces chorizo or your favorite spicy link
    sausage, sliced
8 flour tortillas, 12 inches in diameter
½ yellow onion, minced
2 tablespoons olive oil
8 eggs, beaten
2 garlic cloves, minced
1 teaspoon ground cumin
1 teaspoon freshly ground black pepper
¾ cup chopped fresh cilantro
8 ounces sharp cheddar cheese, grated
    (2 cups)
toppings such as sour cream, guacamole,
    and salsa

In a 12" Dutch oven or skillet, heat sliced sausage, then drain all fat and juice. Remove from pan and set aside, keeping warm. Heat tortillas on inverted Dutch oven lid. Set aside. Add oil to the Dutch oven and sauté onion until translucent. Add eggs, garlic, cumin, and pepper and cook until eggs are nearly done. Add cilantro and serve on tortillas, offering sausage, cheese, and other toppings.

Yield: 8 servings

VEGETABLE EGG CUPS

oil for greasing pan
6 frozen puff pastry shells
6 ounces cheddar cheese, grated
    (1½ cups)
3 tablespoons unbleached all-purpose flour
3 eggs, lightly beaten
¼ cup chopped fresh mushrooms
¼ cup chopped zucchini
3 tablespoons chopped onion
6 crisply cooked bacon slices, crumbled
½ teaspoon salt
dash black pepper

These are delicious served for breakfast or brunch.

Lightly grease 6 muffin cups, or use paper muffin cups.

Roll out each pastry shell into a 6- to 8-inch circle. Line each muffin cup with a circle of dough, so that the edges of the dough stand up at least a half inch above the cup edge.

Toss cheese with flour. Add eggs, mushrooms, zucchini, onion, bacon, salt, and pepper, and mix well. Fill the cups with the cheese mixture.

Bake in Dutch oven for 35 to 40 minutes. For conventional oven, bake at 350°F for 50 minutes.

Yield: 6 servings

BLUEBERRY COBBLER

Filling
4 cups fresh blueberries
5 tablespoons sugar
¾ cup orange juice

Topping
1 cup unbleached all-purpose flour
½ teaspoon baking powder
⅛ teaspoon salt
1 cup (2 sticks) unsalted butter, softened
1 cup sugar
1 egg, well-beaten
½ teaspoon vanilla extract

Cobblers have always been a favorite of the Dutch oven cook, and this one is exceptional. You can also serve this for dessert with a topping of vanilla ice cream.

Mix blueberries, 5 tablespoons sugar, and orange juice. Pour in a 12" Dutch oven or 9" × 13" baking pan and set aside.

Make the topping: Mix the flour, baking powder, and salt in a small bowl and set aside. Mix the butter and the 1 cup of sugar until well blended. Stir in egg and vanilla; then stir in flour mixture. Drop topping by the tablespoonful on top of the blueberry mixture.

Bake in Dutch oven for 30 to 40 minutes, or in 350°F conventional oven for 40 to 45 minutes, until cobbler topping is golden brown and filling is bubbly. Cool slightly before serving.

Yield: 8 to 10 servings

BREAKFAST QUESADILLAS

Salsa

4 plum tomatoes, quartered lengthwise and
thinly sliced
1 small zucchini, quartered lengthwise and
thinly sliced
⅔ yellow bell pepper, diced
4 scallions, thinly sliced
2 jalapeño peppers, seeded and minced
2 tablespoons minced cilantro
4 teaspoons lime juice, or more to taste
½ teaspoon lime zest
cayenne pepper to taste
¼ teaspoon salt

Assembly

4 flour tortillas (8-inch diameter)
2 ounces Monterey Jack cheese, very finely
grated (½ cup)
4 tablespoons sour cream
cilantro sprigs for garnish

For a less spicy quesadilla, use smaller amounts of jalapeño and cayenne pepper.

Make the salsa: Stir together tomatoes, zucchini, yellow pepper, scallions, jalapeño, cilantro, lime juice and zest, cayenne pepper, and salt.

Warm a tortilla in a skillet for 1 to 2 minutes. Turn tortilla and spoon one-quarter of the salsa over half of it. Top salsa with one-quarter of the cheese, fold tortilla over filling, and cook until salsa is heated through and cheese has melted, 2 to 3 minutes. Transfer quesadilla to plate and keep warm in Dutch oven. Repeat with other tortillas. Serve topped with sour cream and sprigs of cilantro.

Yield: 4 servings

CREEK BANK SPUDS

1 pound bacon, cooked and drained
   (reserve ⅛ cup of the fat)
4 potatoes, unpeeled, parboiled, and cut
   into chunks
1½ onions, chopped
2 tablespoons unsalted butter, melted
salt and freshly ground black pepper to taste

Crumble cooked bacon. Combine potatoes, onions, and bacon with butter and reserved bacon fat. Add salt and pepper to taste. Spread across bottom of a Dutch oven or 9″ × 11″ casserole dish.

Bake in Dutch oven for 20 minutes, or in 350°F conventional oven for 30 minutes.

Yield: 4 servings

WILDERNESS EGGS

1 to 2 tablespoons olive oil
½ cup chopped onion
1 small green bell pepper, cored, seeded,
   and diced
1 cup diced celery
2 teaspoons chopped jalapeño pepper
4 cups crushed canned tomatoes
1 small bay leaf
1½ cups soft bread crumbs
kosher salt and freshly ground black pepper
   to taste
8 ounces sharp cheddar cheese, grated
   (2 cups)
8 eggs

Heat a 12″ Dutch oven or large skillet over medium heat and add oil. Add the onion, green pepper, celery, and jalapeño; cook, stirring until softened but not browned, 4 to 5 minutes. Add tomatoes and bay leaf; simmer until the tomatoes have reduced and most of the liquid has evaporated, 20 to 30 minutes. Remove Dutch oven or pan from heat and stir in the bread crumbs. Season to taste with salt and pepper.

Spread one half of the sauce on the bottom of a 12″ Dutch oven or 9-inch square baking dish, removing bay leaf. Sprinkle 1 cup cheese on top. Scoop the rest of the tomato sauce over the cheese; top with the rest of the cheese. With the back of a large spoon, make 8 depressions the size of an egg and crack an egg into each well.

Bake until whites of eggs are set and yolks are still a little runny, 15 to 25 minutes. For a conventional oven, bake at 350°F.

Yield: 8 servings

JOE BUMP BACON AND EGG SANDWICH

6 English muffins, split
4 tablespoons unsalted butter
8 bacon slices
6 large eggs
salt and freshly ground black pepper to taste
2 bunches arugula

Joe Bump was a prospector and packer from Cascade, Idaho, who moved into a cabin that was built by some other prospectors in the 1930s. Said to have been a sheriff in the Black Hills country of South Dakota, Joe had to move to Cascade after losing his toes to frostbite in a Bear Valley snowstorm. He was known among the miners for his bacon and egg sandwich. Serve this as a brunch or even supper with hash brown potatoes and a marinated artichoke heart and cherry tomato salad.

Toast muffins and spread with 3 tablespoons of butter. Arrange bottom halves on six plates. Cook bacon slices in Dutch oven or heavy skillet over medium-high heat until brown and crisp. Transfer bacon to paper towel to drain. Arrange bacon slices atop muffin bottoms.

Pour drippings from skillet; melt remaining butter over medium-high until foamy. Crack eggs into Dutch oven or skillet. Cover and cook eggs to desired doneness; sprinkle with salt and pepper. Transfer eggs to each muffin bottom. Place arugula on each and cover with muffin top.

Yield: 6 servings

CHILAQUILES

1 cup chopped red onion
½ cup chopped tomato
1 cup chopped Swiss chard
1 tablespoon vegetable oil
½ cup cooked corn
½ cup cooked black beans, drained and
    rinsed if canned
1 cup shredded cooked chicken
½ cup chicken broth
1 cup enchilada sauce (not salsa)
1 tablespoon chopped fresh parsley
2 tablespoons chopped cilantro
4 cups tortilla chips
1 teaspoon salt
½ teaspoon freshly ground black pepper
6 ounces mild cheddar cheese, grated
    (1½ cups)

In a large skillet, sauté onion, tomato, and chard in oil. Add corn, beans, and chicken and cook until heated through.

Stir in broth, enchilada sauce, parsley, and cilantro until blended. Add tortilla chips, salt, and pepper, cover, and cook, stirring occasionally, until chips begin to soften, about 5 minutes.

Transfer mixture to a 10″ Dutch oven and top with cheese; with the lid covered with charcoal, heat until cheese bubbles, about 3 minutes. For conventional cooking, leave mixture in skillet; cover with cheese and heat over medium heat for about 3 minutes, until cheese bubbles.

Yield: 4 servings

EGGS ELEGANT

½ teaspoon salt
¼ teaspoon black pepper
1 tablespoon dry mustard
2 cans (10½ ounces each) cream of
    chicken soup
1 cup milk
8 ounces grated cheddar cheese (2 cups)
1 package (10 ounces) frozen asparagus
    pieces, thawed and drained
8 eggs
4 whole wheat English muffins

Combine salt, pepper, dry mustard, cream of chicken soup, and milk in Dutch oven or saucepan. Stir over medium heat until smooth and creamy. Stir in cheese until melted. Add asparagus pieces.

If cooking in Dutch oven, make hollows for six to eight eggs; break an egg into each hollow. For conventional cooking, pour egg mixture into 9″ × 11″ casserole dish.

Bake in Dutch oven for 15 to 20 minutes, or in conventional oven at 350°F for 30 minutes (or until eggs are set to your liking).

Cut English muffins in half and toast. Serve eggs over English muffins, one egg to each half.

Yield: 8 servings

BREAKFAST POLENTA WITH CHORIZO

1¾ cups crumbled queso fresco or feta
    cheese
¾ cup chopped fresh cilantro
3½ cups water
1¼ cups polenta (coarse yellow cornmeal)
    or regular cornmeal
16 ounces frozen corn kernels, thawed
salt and black pepper to taste
1 pound fresh link chorizo or your favorite
    spicy sausage, casings removed
1 pound cherry tomatoes

Serve this with fried or poached eggs for brunch or breakfast.

Combine cheese and cilantro. Set aside. Mix water, polenta, and corn kernels in a 12″ Dutch oven or 9″ × 13″ glass baking dish. Sprinkle generously with salt and pepper and stir to blend well. Bake until water is absorbed and polenta is tender, 25 to 30 minutes, stirring once. For a conventional oven, bake at 425°F.

Meanwhile, sauté chorizo in Dutch oven or heavy large skillet over medium-high heat until browned, about 6 minutes, breaking it into small pieces. Add tomatoes. Cover, reduce heat to medium, and simmer until soft, about 6 minutes. Uncover; crush some tomatoes with fork. Simmer until tomatoes release juices and sauce thickens slightly, about 10 minutes. Spoon polenta onto plates. Top with chorizo mixture and then cheese mixture.

Yield: 6 servings

ROCKY'S SMOKED HAM, ARTICHOKE, MONTRACHET CHEESE STRATA

unsalted butter for greasing pan
2 cups milk
¼ cup olive oil
8 cups 1-inch cubes sourdough bread,
    crusts trimmed
1½ cups whipping cream
5 large eggs
1 tablespoon chopped garlic
1½ teaspoons salt
¾ teaspoon black pepper
½ teaspoon ground nutmeg
12 ounces crumbled Montrachet cheese
2 tablespoons chopped fresh sage
1 tablespoon chopped fresh thyme
12 ounces smoked ham, chopped
3 jars (6½-ounces each) marinated
    artichoke hearts, drained, halved
    lengthwise
1 cup (packed) grated Fontina cheese
1½ cups (packed) grated Parmesan cheese

This strata (which means layered) is great for Christmas morning or another special occasion—it is assembled a day ahead and baked just before serving. Mimosas are a nice addition to the menu.

Butter a 12″ Dutch oven or a 9″ × 13″ glass baking dish. Whisk milk and oil in large bowl. Stir in bread. Let stand until liquid is absorbed, about 10 minutes.

Whisk cream, eggs, garlic, salt, pepper, and nutmeg together in another large bowl to blend. Add Montrachet cheese. Set aside. Combine sage and thyme in small bowl.

Place half of bread mixture in prepared Dutch oven or dish. Top with half of ham, artichoke hearts, herbs, and cheeses. Pour half of cream mixture over. Repeat layering with remaining bread, ham, artichoke hearts, herbs, cheeses, and cream mixture.

Bake until firm in center and brown around edges, about 1 hour. For conventional oven, bake at 350°F for 1 hour 15 minutes.

Yield: 8 servings

POSH POTATO AND SAUSAGE BREAKFAST

6 medium red-skinned potatoes, quartered
2 tablespoons olive oil
1 medium onion, diced
2 large scallions, sliced crosswise
1 large tomato, chopped
1 tablespoon minced fresh basil
¼ teaspoon dried oregano
⅛ teaspoon dried thyme
salt and freshly ground black pepper to taste
¾ pound bulk sausage
4 ounces cheddar cheese, grated (1 cup)
4 ounces sour cream
½ teaspoon paprika

Boil the potatoes until tender.

Heat oil and sauté potatoes until lightly browned, about 10 minutes. Add onion, scallions, tomato, basil, oregano, thyme, and salt and pepper; sauté until onions are tender and set aside.

Brown sausage; drain. Toss sausage with potato mixture and transfer to Dutch oven or 2-quart casserole dish.

Bake for 5 minutes in Dutch oven, or 10 minutes in 350°F conventional oven. Sprinkle cheese on top, and bake until cheese is bubbly, about 10 minutes. Top with sour cream, sprinkle with paprika, and serve.

Yield: 4 servings

DUTCH OVEN SAUSAGE AND POTATOES

2 tablespoons plus 1 tablespoon olive oil
6 unpeeled red-skinned potatoes, cut into
     ½-inch cubes
2 medium onions, chopped
½ pound fully cooked smoked turkey
     sausage, sliced ¼-inch thick on the
     diagonal
2 tablespoons fresh thyme (or 1 teaspoon
     dried)
1½ to 2 teaspoons cumin seed, slightly
     crushed
¼ teaspoon salt
¼ teaspoon black pepper

Heat 2 tablespoons of the oil in a large skillet or Dutch oven. Cook potatoes and onion, uncovered, for about 12 minutes or until potatoes are nearly tender, stirring occasionally.

Add sausage and the remaining 1 tablespoon of oil and cook, stirring often, about 10 minutes longer until potatoes and onions are tender and slightly brown. Stir in thyme, cumin, salt, and pepper.

Yield: 6 servings

BACON AND LEEK PIE

pastry for 9-inch single-crust pie (see recipe on page 161)
2 tablespoons unsalted butter
2 cups chopped leeks
¼ cup chopped fresh parsley
1 teaspoon unbleached all-purpose flour
6 slices uncooked bacon, cut into ½-inch pieces
3 large eggs
⅔ cup whipping cream
⅓ cup milk
¼ teaspoon salt
¼ teaspoon black pepper
⅛ teaspoon nutmeg

Prepare pie crust according to recipe. Place crust in Dutch oven and press up sides at least 1 inch, folding excess over to form double edges, or place in 9" pie dish. Pierce crust bottom all over with fork and bake until pale golden (at 350°F in conventional oven), about 10 minutes.

Melt butter in a skillet, add leeks and parsley, and sauté until soft. Stir in flour. Spoon mixture onto crust.

Cook bacon until crisp and drain. Sprinkle bacon over leeks.

In a separate bowl, beat eggs, cream, milk, salt, pepper, and nutmeg and pour into crust. Bake in Dutch oven about 25 minutes, or in 350°F conventional oven for 45 to 50 minutes, until set in center.

Yield: 6 servings

ROCKY MOUNTAIN EGGS

2 tablespoons plus 4 tablespoons unsalted butter or margarine
2 small potatoes, cut into ½-inch cubes
1 large onion, finely chopped
8 ounces ground spicy turkey sausage
2 tablespoons chopped fresh parsley
6 eggs
½ teaspoon salt
freshly ground black pepper to taste
1 tablespoon milk
2 ounces Monterey Jack cheese, grated (½ cup)

This breakfast surprise turns scrambled eggs into a sturdy entree.

Heat 2 tablespoons butter in Dutch oven. Sauté potatoes, onion, and sausage for about 15 minutes until sausage is browned evenly and potatoes are tender. Sprinkle with parsley and dot with 4 tablespoons butter, and reduce heat.

In a separate bowl, beat eggs with salt, pepper, and milk. Pour into Dutch oven over cooked ingredients and cook, lifting set portion with a spatula to let uncooked egg flow underneath. When nearly set, sprinkle with cheese and cover until cheese melts. Cut into wedges to serve.

Yield: 4 to 6 servings

FAMOUS-ON-TWO-CONTINENTS PANCAKES

1 cup whole wheat flour
1 cup unbleached all-purpose flour
1 teaspoon baking powder
½ teaspoon salt
1 teaspoon ground cinnamon
¼ to ⅓ cup brown sugar (to taste)
½ cup roasted sunflower seeds and/or
   raisins
dash vanilla extract
2 tablespoons vegetable oil
1 cup (or so) of one of the following: ginger
   ale, beer, milk, pineapple juice, coconut
   milk, or fruit juice of your choice
1 egg, lightly beaten (optional)
2 small bananas (or 1 very large), mashed

John Caccia, owner of Idaho Bolo, Etc., in Ketchum, Idaho, and a seasoned river guide, adopted this pancake recipe while living in Australia. There, the pancakes are called "pikelets."

Mix wheat flour, all-purpose flour, baking powder, salt, cinnamon, brown sugar, and sunflower seeds and/or raisins. Add vanilla, vegetable oil, and chosen liquid (with egg, if desired) and stir. Stir banana(s) into batter.

Cook on seasoned griddle. You can also use a Dutch oven lid as a griddle. Serve with your favorite toppings.

Yield: about 15 4-inch pancakes

SOURDOUGH PANCAKES

1 cup Sourdough Starter (recipe on page 56)
2½ cups unbleached all-purpose flour
2 cups lukewarm water
2 eggs, beaten
3 tablespoons vegetable oil plus more for
    greasing griddle
½ teaspoon salt
1½ teaspoons baking soda
¼ cup buttermilk
1 pint fresh blueberries, washed and drained
    (optional)

The night before, place the starter in a large glass bowl. Pour in flour and water and mix until smooth. Cover the bowl and place it in a draft-free place overnight.

When you are ready to prepare the pancakes, add the eggs, oil, salt, baking soda, and buttermilk to starter. Mix well and let rest for 10 minutes. Then add blueberries, if desired.

Lightly oil griddle. Pour batter ¼ cup at a time and cook cakes for 2 to 3 minutes, or until small bubbles form on them. Turn and cook 1 to 2 minutes longer. Serve with your favorite toppings.

Yield: about 15 4-inch pancakes

GINGERBREAD CORN CAKES

1 cup whole wheat flour
¼ cup unbleached all-purpose flour
¼ cup yellow cornmeal
2½ teaspoons baking powder
1 teaspoon ground ginger
½ teaspoon ground cinnamon
½ teaspoon ground cloves
½ teaspoon nutmeg
½ teaspoon salt
¼ cup molasses
1¾ cups milk
¼ cup vegetable oil plus more for greasing
    griddle
2 eggs, beaten

These soft, spicy hotcakes are delicious eaten with apples in any form. Top with a mound of sweetened whipped cream or yogurt cheese and a dash of nutmeg.

Mix whole wheat flour, all-purpose flour, cornmeal, baking powder, ginger, cinnamon, cloves, nutmeg, salt, and molasses. Make a well in the center of mixture and set aside.

Whisk the milk and oil with the beaten eggs. Pour into well in dry ingredients. Mix just until smooth. The batter will be thin to start with but will thicken as it stands. Let rest 5 minutes.

Lightly oil griddle. Pour batter ¼ cup at a time and cook cakes for 2 to 3 minutes, or until small bubbles form on them. Turn and cook 1 to 2 minutes longer.

Yield: about 10 4-inch pancakes

KLINKHAMMER COFFEE CAKE

Cake
1¼ cups brown sugar
2½ cups whole wheat flour
1 tablespoon baking powder
¼ teaspoon baking soda
¼ teaspoon salt
½ cup (1 stick) unsalted butter
3 eggs, lightly beaten
1 cup milk
1 teaspoon vanilla extract
1 cup plain yogurt

Topping
¼ cup butter, melted
¾ cup chopped walnuts
¾ cup brown sugar
1½ teaspoons ground cinnamon
¾ cup raisins

Charlie Shepp and Peter Klinkhammer purchased Shepp Ranch on the Main Salmon River in Idaho in the early 1900s. Pete spent nearly fifty years on this ranch, selling it in 1950 for $10,000—ten times what was paid for it.

Line Dutch oven or 9″ × 11″ baking pan with parchment paper, extending paper two inches up sides and set aside.

Mix brown sugar, whole wheat flour, baking powder, baking soda, and salt.

In a separate dish, melt butter, then add beaten eggs, milk, vanilla, and yogurt. Make a well in the dry ingredients and pour in the liquids. Mix only to moisten the dry ingredients. Pour batter into Dutch oven or pan.

Partially bake batter in Dutch oven for 25 minutes, or in 350°F conventional oven for 35 minutes, before adding topping.

While batter is baking, make the topping: Stir together melted butter, walnuts, brown sugar, cinnamon, and raisins.

After initial baking time, sprinkle topping mixture on top of cake and bake another 5 to 10 minutes or until a knife inserted into the center comes out nearly clean. Cool slightly before slicing.

Yield: 10 to 12 servings

APPLE-CINNAMON BROWN BETTY

unsalted butter for greasing pan plus
    1 cup (2 sticks), melted
2 cups rolled oats
2 cups unbleached all-purpose flour
2 cups brown sugar
2 teaspoons ground cinnamon
½ teaspoon baking powder
2 tablespoons cornstarch
5 tablespoons fresh lemon juice
    (about 2 large lemons)
6 cups apples, peeled and sliced

This great breakfast dish can also be served as a dessert topped with whipped cream or ice cream. Try making it with peaches instead of apples.

Grease a 12″ Dutch oven or 9″ × 13″ baking pan and set aside.

Mix butter, oats, flour, brown sugar, cinnamon, and baking powder. Set aside.

In a separate large bowl, mix cornstarch and lemon juice. Add apples and toss to coat with juice mixture. Sprinkle one-third of the oatmeal mixture over the bottom of Dutch oven or baking pan. Spread apple mixture in an even layer on top. Sprinkle remaining oatmeal mixture evenly over apples.

Bake in Dutch oven for about 30 minutes, or in 350°F conventional oven for about 35 to 40 minutes, until topping is light golden brown. Cut into squares and serve warm.

Yield: 12 servings

HUEVOS MIDDLE FORK

1 teaspoon plus 2 tablespoons corn oil
6 corn tortillas, cut in half
12 eggs
4 large scallions, sliced
2 fresh jalapeño peppers, very thinly sliced
½ red bell pepper, diced
¼ cup chopped cilantro
1½ teaspoons ground cumin
4 ounces feta cheese, crumbled
salt and black pepper to taste
cilantro sprigs for garnish

Heat 1 teaspoon oil, add tortilla halves, and fry until golden brown and crisp. Transfer to paper towels and drain.

Beat together eggs, scallions, jalapeño and bell peppers, cilantro, cumin, and half of the cheese. Crumble in four tortilla halves. Season to taste with salt and pepper. Let stand 5 minutes.

Heat 2 tablespoons oil and add egg mixture. Cook until just set, stirring frequently. Sprinkle with remaining cheese. Stand two tortilla halves in each serving and garnish with cilantro sprigs.

Yield: 4 servings

BLUEBERRY CINNAMON BROWN BETTY

unsalted butter for greasing pan plus 1 cup
  (2 sticks), melted
2 cups rolled oats
2 cups unbleached all-purpose flour
2 cups brown sugar
2 teaspoons ground cinnamon
½ teaspoon baking powder
2 tablespoons cornstarch
5 tablespoons fresh lemon juice
  (need about 2 large lemons)
3½ pints fresh blueberries, rinsed and
  picked over

This also makes a great dessert topped with ice cream. Equivalent amounts of sliced apples, peaches, or pitted cherries can be substituted for the blueberries.

Grease a 12″ Dutch oven or 9″ × 13″ baking pan and set aside.

Mix butter, oats, flour, brown sugar, cinnamon, and baking powder in large bowl and set aside.

In a separate large bowl, mix cornstarch and lemon juice. Add blueberries and toss to coat.

Sprinkle one-third of the oatmeal mixture over the bottom of Dutch oven or baking pan. Spread all the blueberries in an even layer on top. Sprinkle remaining oatmeal mixture evenly over blueberries.

Bake in Dutch oven for about 30 minutes, or in 350°F conventional oven for about 35 to 40 minutes, until topping is light golden brown. Cut into squares and serve warm.

Yield: 12 servings

SINFULLY SUMPTUOUS STICKY BUNS

Buns

2 packages active dry yeast
½ cup warm water
2 cups warm milk
½ cup vegetable shortening
6 tablespoons sugar
2 teaspoons salt
2 eggs
6½ cups unbleached all-purpose flour

Caramel Glaze

1 cup (2 sticks) unsalted butter
3 cups brown sugar
½ cup light corn syrup
3 cups broken pecan or walnut pieces

The seductive flavors of caramel and sweet butter and the crunch of nuts make these buns the highlight of any breakfast or brunch.

Dissolve the yeast in the warm water.

In a large bowl, mix milk, shortening, sugar, salt, and eggs until well blended. Add the yeast and 4 cups of the flour; mix vigorously. Add the rest of the flour to make a soft dough. Knead for 1 minute. Let dough rest for 10 minute; then knead again until the dough is smooth and elastic. Cover it and let rise until it doubles in bulk.

Make the caramel glaze: Put butter, brown sugar, and corn syrup in a saucepan. Heat and stir until the butter is melted and the sugar dissolved. Remove from heat and pour 1 cup of glaze into a small bowl and set aside. Spread the remaining glaze over the bottom of a 12″ Dutch oven or 9″ × 12″ baking pan and sprinkle nuts over the glaze.

Roll out the dough into a rectangle and spread with glaze. Roll up like a jelly roll from the wide side into a long tube. Cut into 1½-inch pieces. Place each piece in the Dutch oven, flat side down. Cover and let rise until puffy.

Bake in Dutch oven for 25 to 30 minutes, or in 350°F conventional oven for 30 to 35 minutes. Invert pan onto waxed paper. Serve warm.

Yield: 12 large buns

APPLESAUCE-OATMEAL MUFFINS

Applesauce adds extra moistness to these whole-grain muffins.

Line bottom of Dutch oven with 12 paper muffin cups, or line 12 medium-sized muffin cups with paper baking cups.

Combine oats, flour, ¾ teaspoon cinnamon, baking powder, and baking soda in a large bowl. Blend in applesauce, skim milk, ½ cup brown sugar, vegetable oil, and egg white, and mix until dry ingredients are moistened. Fill muffin cups two-thirds full.

Make the topping: Combine oats, 1 tablespoon brown sugar, ¼ teaspoon cinnamon, and butter. Sprinkle over batter.

Bake muffins in Dutch oven for 20 minutes, or in 400°F conventional oven for 20 minutes, or until deep golden brown.

Yield: about 1 dozen

Muffins

1½ cups rolled oats
1¼ cups unbleached all-purpose flour
¾ teaspoon ground cinnamon
1 tablespoon baking powder
¾ tablespoon baking soda
1 cup unsweetened applesauce
½ cup skim milk
½ cup brown sugar
3 tablespoons vegetable oil
1 egg white

Topping

¼ cup oats
1 tablespoon brown sugar
¼ teaspoon ground cinnamon
1 tablespoon unsalted butter, melted

SAVORY SAWTOOTH BISCUITS

4 cups unbleached all-purpose flour plus
     more for rolling out dough
3 tablespoons sugar
2 tablespoons baking powder
2 teaspoons chopped fresh sage
2 teaspoons chopped fresh chives
pinch of kosher salt
1 cup (2 sticks) salted butter, cut into pieces
2 cups heavy cream

*Fresh sage and chives add a savory taste to a basic biscuit recipe.
Spread them with soft butter when they are piping hot! Delicious
with the Wilderness Eggs.*

Combine flour, sugar, baking powder, sage, chives, and salt in a
bowl or food processor. Add the butter and pulse on and off or
cut with fork or pastry cutter until dough resembles coarse meal.
Add the cream all at once and pulse a few times or stir with fork,
until the dough comes together in a ball.

Place the dough on a lightly floured surface and gently pat
into a 1-inch thick round. With a 2- to 3-inch biscuit cutter or
the like, cut out rounds and place on the bottom of a 12″ Dutch
oven or on an ungreased cookie sheet. Press scraps together and
cut out additional biscuits.

Bake until biscuits are golden brown, about 20 minutes. For
conventional oven, bake at 400°F.

Yield: 12 biscuits

Breads

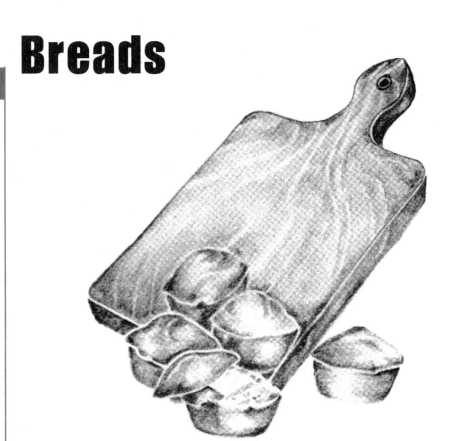

Remember

When a recipe calls for baking, braising, stewing, or roasting, the Dutch oven must be covered with charcoal briquettes on top of the lid. For boiling, frying, sautéing, and quick heating, leave the Dutch oven cover off. For more on cooking techniques for the Dutch oven, see "Dutch Oven Care and Use," pages 2–4. When using a conventional oven, preheat the oven to the given baking temperature.

CORN BREAD

unsalted butter for greasing pan plus
    2 tablespoons
1¾ cups yellow cornmeal
¼ cup whole wheat flour
¼ cup powdered milk
3 tablespoons baking powder
1 teaspoon sea salt
1 egg, lightly beaten
1 tablespoon honey
1½ cups milk

Butter a Dutch oven or 9″ × 9″ baking pan.

Combine cornmeal, flour, powdered milk, baking powder, and salt. Add egg, honey, butter, and milk, and stir until moist. Pour batter into Dutch oven or pan.

Bake in Dutch oven for 20 minutes, or in 425°F conventional oven for 20 to 25 minutes.

Yield: 6 servings

NO-KNEAD OATMEAL BREAD

unsalted butter for greasing pans and
    rising bowl
2 cups boiling water
1 cup rolled oats
⅓ cup vegetable shortening
½ cup light molasses (or honey)
1 tablespoon salt
2 packages active dry yeast
2 eggs, lightly beaten
6½ cups whole wheat flour
flour for rolling out dough

Butter a bowl *or* two Dutch ovens; if cooking conventionally, butter a bowl *and* two loaf pans.

Combine boiling water, oats, shortening, molasses or honey, and salt. Cool to lukewarm. Add yeast and mix well. Blend in eggs. Gradually add flour, mixing until dough is well blended. Place dough in greased bowl or Dutch oven and cover; let rise until double. (If you want to bake the dough later in the day, you may put it in a refrigerator or cold place for several hours.)

Shape dough into two loaves on a well-floured board and place in two loaf pans covered with damp towels or plastic wrap, or in two covered Dutch ovens. Let rise in warm place until doubled in bulk, about 2 hours.

Bake in Dutch oven for 45 minutes, or in 350°F conventional oven for 1 hour.

Yield: 2 loaves

SOUR CREAM–BUTTERMILK CORN BREAD

unsalted butter for greasing pan
2 cups white cornmeal
3½ teaspoons baking powder
½ teaspoon baking soda
dash salt
1½ cups low-fat sour cream
2 eggs, lightly beaten
2 tablespoons olive oil
⅔ cup buttermilk

Butter a 12″ Dutch oven or 9″ × 12″ baking pan.

Combine cornmeal, baking powder, baking soda, and salt.

In a separate bowl, lightly beat together sour cream, eggs, olive oil, and buttermilk. Combine gently with the dry ingredients; do not overmix. Pour batter into Dutch oven or pan.

Bake for 30 minutes in Dutch oven, or 30 to 35 minutes in 375°F conventional oven, until lightly browned. This is delicious served with Saucy Chicken (recipe on page 76).

Yield: 6 servings

DILLY CASSEROLE BREAD

1 package active dry yeast
¼ cup warm water (105°F to 115°F)
1 cup creamed cottage cheese
1 tablespoon granulated sugar
1 tablespoon dried, minced onion
1 tablespoon unsalted butter
1 teaspoon dried dill
1 teaspoon salt
¼ teaspoon baking soda
1 egg
2½ cups unbleached all-purpose flour

Add yeast to water to soften.

In a mixing bowl combine cottage cheese, sugar, onion, butter, dill, salt, baking soda, and egg. Add softened yeast. Add flour and beat well. Cover. Let rise until double in size.

Punch down batter. (Batter will be sticky.) Turn into buttered 10″ or 12″ Dutch oven.

Bake for 40 to 50 minutes or until it has formed a nice crust and is golden brown on top and bottom. For conventional oven, bake in a casserole at 350°F for 45 to 50 minutes.

Yield: 6 to 8 servings

OATMEAL-BUTTERMILK BREAD

1 cup plus 1 tablespoon quick-cooking oats
1½ cups unbleached all-purpose flour
½ cup whole wheat flour
1 teaspoon baking powder
½ teaspoon baking soda
½ teaspoon salt
1 cup buttermilk
¼ cup canola oil
¼ cup molasses
1 egg

Line a 10″ Dutch oven or 9″ × 12″ baking pan with parchment paper, extending the paper 2 inches up sides.

Toast 1 cup of oats in separate Dutch oven for about 15 minutes, or toast on baking sheet in 450°F conventional oven for 10 minutes. Combine toasted oats, all-purpose flour, wheat flour, baking powder, baking soda, and salt, and stir well. Make a well in center of mixture.

In a separate bowl, combine buttermilk, oil, molasses, and egg. Pour into dry ingredients and stir just until moistened. Spoon batter into Dutch oven or pan. Sprinkle with the remaining oats.

Bake for 40 to 50 minutes in Dutch oven, or 35 to 40 minutes in 350°F conventional oven, or until a toothpick inserted in the center comes out clean.

Yield: 8 servings

ANGIE'S CHEESE CRACKERS

unsalted butter for greasing pan plus ½ cup
1 cup unbleached all-purpose flour
¼ teaspoon baking soda
½ teaspoon salt
½ cup cornmeal
¼ cup wheat germ
2 ounces cheddar cheese, grated (½ cup)
¼ cup milk
1 tablespoon vinegar

My sister-in-law, Angie Mills Cochran, shared this recipe with me.

Liberally grease a Dutch oven or baking sheet and set aside.

Combine all other ingredients. Roll dough out to about ¼-inch thickness and pat into bottom of Dutch oven or onto baking sheet. Score lines with a fork for breaking.

Bake in Dutch oven for 15 to 20 minutes, or in 400°F conventional oven for 15 to 20 minutes, until golden brown. Cool and break along scored lines.

Yield: 12 crackers

BANANA-CARROT BREAD

unsalted butter for greasing pan
1 cup whole wheat flour
1 cup unbleached all-purpose flour
1 teaspoon baking powder
1 teaspoon baking soda
½ teaspoon ground cinnamon
¼ teaspoon salt
⅛ teaspoon ground cloves
¼ cup margarine
¾ cup brown sugar
3 eggs, lightly beaten
2 large, very ripe bananas, peeled
     and mashed
1¼ teaspoons vanilla extract
2 large carrots, finely grated
½ cup chopped walnuts

Butter a 12″ Dutch oven or loaf pan.

In a large bowl, combine flours, baking powder, baking soda, cinnamon, salt, and cloves and set aside.

In a medium bowl, cream margarine and brown sugar. Beat in eggs, bananas, and vanilla. Add banana mixture to dry ingredients until just blended. Stir in carrots and walnuts. Pour into Dutch oven or pan.

Bake for 1 hour in Dutch oven, or 55 to 60 minutes in 350°F conventional oven, or until a knife inserted in the center of the loaf comes out clean.

Yield: 1 loaf

BIG BEND BANANA-WALNUT BREAD

1 cup unbleached all-purpose flour
1 cup whole wheat flour
1 cup brown sugar
1 tablespoon baking powder
1 teaspoon ground cinnamon
¼ teaspoon baking soda
4 egg whites
1 cup-mashed bananas
½ cup buttermilk
⅓ cup applesauce
1 teaspoon vanilla extract
½ cup chopped walnuts

Line a 12″ Dutch oven or loaf pan with parchment paper, extending the paper 2 inches up sides.

In a large bowl, combine all-purpose flour, wheat flour, brown sugar, baking powder, cinnamon, and baking soda and set aside.

Beat egg whites until foamy. Add bananas, buttermilk, applesauce, and vanilla. Stir into dry ingredients until just blended. Add walnuts. Pour into Dutch oven or pan.

Bake in Dutch oven for 45 to 55 minutes, or in 375°F conventional oven for 45 minutes, until golden.

Yield: 12 servings

ZUCCHINI BREAD

unsalted butter for greasing pan
flour for dusting pan
3 cups whole wheat flour
1 teaspoon salt
1 teaspoon ground cinnamon
1 teaspoon ginger
1 teaspoon baking soda
¼ teaspoon baking powder
1 cup chopped walnuts
3 eggs
1 cup honey
1 cup vegetable oil
3 teaspoons vanilla extract
2 cups washed and grated zucchini
   (unpeeled)

Butter and flour two 10″ Dutch ovens or two loaf pans.

In a large bowl, mix flour, salt, cinnamon, ginger, baking soda, baking powder, and walnuts.

In a separate bowl, mix eggs, honey, and oil. Blend in vanilla and grated zucchini. Mix wet ingredients into dry. Pour batter into Dutch ovens or loaf pans.

Bake in Dutch ovens for about 1 hour, turning oven every 15 minutes, or in a 325°F conventional oven for 1 hour. Bread is done when a knife inserted in the center comes out clean. Remove from pan and let cool before slicing.

Yield: 2 loaves

BRAN-WHEAT MUFFINS

1 cup unbleached all-purpose flour
1 cup whole wheat flour
¾ cup whole bran cereal
3 teaspoons baking powder
½ teaspoon salt
1 egg
¼ cup oil or unsalted butter, melted; plus
    more for greasing muffin cups, unless
    using paper liners
4 tablespoons honey
1 cup milk

Mix all-purpose flour, wheat flour, cereal, baking powder, and salt. Form a well in the center of the mixture.

In a separate bowl, lightly beat the egg and stir in oil or butter, honey, and milk. Pour all at once into the well in the flour mixture. Stir to just moisten ingredients, scraping the bottom of the bowl as you stir. Batter should look lumpy.

Grease cups of one 12-muffin tin or line them with paper baking cups or, if using a Dutch oven, line the bottom with twelve paper baking cups. Fill each muffin cup two-thirds full with batter.

Bake in Dutch oven for 15 to 20 minutes, or in a 375°F conventional oven for about 25 minutes, until well browned. Serve muffins hot with butter or honey.

Yield: 1 dozen

PARMESAN PUFFS

unsalted butter for greasing pan plus ¼ cup
¼ cup milk
¼ cup water
¼ teaspoon salt
½ cup unbleached all-purpose flour
2 large eggs
4 ounces Parmesan cheese, grated (1 cup)
freshly ground black pepper to taste

These savory puffs are great as appetizers or served with soup.

Butter a Dutch oven or baking sheet.

Combine milk, water, butter, and salt in a saucepan and bring to a boil. Reduce the heat and add flour. Beat the mixture until it leaves the sides of the pan and forms a ball. Transfer the mixture to a bowl. Whisk in the eggs, one at a time, whisking well after each addition. Stir in Parmesan and pepper.

Drop the batter in eight mounds in Dutch oven or baking pan. Bake the puffs in Dutch oven with a lot of coals on the top, or in 400°F conventional oven, for about 20 minutes, until they are crisp and golden.

Yield: 8 puffs

RICOTTA PUFFS

1 cup low-fat ricotta cheese
3 eggs
¼ cup sugar
1 cup unbleached all-purpose flour
4 teaspoons baking powder
¼ teaspoon salt
24 ounces peanut or canola oil for frying
2 cups confectioners' sugar

Beat ricotta cheese, eggs, and sugar until blended and smooth.

In a separate bowl, blend flour, baking powder, and salt. Beat into cheese to form a smooth, thick batter.

Heat oil in Dutch oven or large kettle. Drop batter by the teaspoonful in the oil, frying several at a time. Fry puffs until golden brown on all sides. Drain well. Dust with confectioners' sugar and serve warm.

Yield: about 3 dozen puffs

PARMESAN POPOVERS

5 egg whites
1⅓ cups milk
3 tablespoons butter, melted, plus more
    for greasing muffin cups, unless using
    paper liners
1⅓ cups unbleached all-purpose flour
1½ teaspoons mixed dried herbs such as
    basil, oregano, and parsley
3 tablespoons grated Parmesan cheese

Mix egg whites, milk, and butter in a large bowl. Stir in flour, herbs, and Parmesan until just combined. Let batter rest for 5 minutes.

Grease a popover or muffin tin, or line Dutch oven with paper muffin cups. Spoon batter into each cup, filling each two-thirds full.

Bake in Dutch oven for 15 minutes. For conventional cooking, bake in 450°F oven for 12 to 15 minutes, reduce heat to 350°F, and bake until popovers are firm and golden brown, 10 to 12 minutes longer. Serve immediately.

Yield: 12 popovers

FOCACCIA FLATS

unsalted butter for greasing pan
flour for rolling out dough
1 loaf frozen bread dough, thawed
¼ cup olive oil
1 teaspoon coarse salt
¼ pound prosciutto, thinly sliced
8 ounces mozzarella cheese, grated
        (2 cups)
1 tablespoon red wine vinegar
⅛ teaspoon crushed dried hot red chilies
⅓ cup finely chopped red onion
2 tablespoons drained capers

Frozen bread dough makes a quick loaf of flat bread, similar to Italian focaccia. Use for pizza-like, hot prosciutto-and-cheese open-faced sandwiches.

Butter a 12″ Dutch oven, or butter a 12-inch circle on a baking sheet. Roll bread dough out into a 12″ circle on a floured table, and ease dough into Dutch oven or onto baking sheet. With fingers, poke deep holes in dough at 2-inch intervals. Brush with 2 tablespoons of the olive oil and sprinkle with coarse salt. Cover and let rise until doubled.

Bake in Dutch oven for 12 to 15 minutes, or in 350°F conventional oven for 20 to 25 minutes, until golden brown. Cover focaccia with prosciutto and cheese.

Stir together remaining oil, vinegar, chilies, onion, and capers. Spoon onion mixture evenly over cheese. Return lid and bake until cheese melts and is lightly browned. Cut into wedges and serve hot.

Yield: 4 to 6 servings

CURRANT SCONES

3 cups unbleached all-purpose flour
3 tablespoons sugar
1 teaspoon baking soda
½ teaspoon salt
6 tablespoons chilled unsalted butter
⅓ cup dried currants
1 egg, lightly beaten
¾ cup plus 3 tablespoons buttermilk
flour for rolling out dough
1 tablespoon milk

Line a 12″ Dutch oven or baking sheet with parchment paper.

Mix flour, sugar, baking soda, and salt in a large bowl. Cut in butter until mixture is like coarse cornmeal. Mix in currants. Mix in egg and buttermilk to form a soft dough.

Turn dough out onto a floured surface. Pat dough into a ¾-inch-thick round. Cut out rounds with a 2½-inch cutter or glass, using all the dough. Put into Dutch oven or on baking sheet and brush tops with milk.

Bake in Dutch oven for about 18 minutes, or in 375°F conventional oven for 20 minutes, until scones are golden brown. Serve warm with butter and jam.

Yield: 15 scones

BAKED CINNAMON SCONES

unsalted butter for greasing pans
2 cups whole wheat flour
1 tablespoon baking powder
1 teaspoon baking soda
1 tablespoon sugar
½ teaspoon salt
½ teaspoon cinnamon
2 tablespoons oil
½ cup buttermilk

Butter a Dutch oven or two baking sheets.

Combine flour, baking powder, baking soda, sugar, salt, and cinnamon in a large bowl. Stir in oil and buttermilk with a fork until mixture clings to itself. Knead dough gently for 3 minutes.

Divide dough into three parts. Roll out each part to ½ inch thick. Cut into six wedges or use a small glass or cutter to cut into 2-inch rounds. Place in Dutch oven or on baking sheets.

Bake in a Dutch oven for 10 to 15 minutes, or in 450°F conventional oven for 10 to 15 minutes. Serve hot.

Yield: 18 scones

CHEDDAR CORNMEAL SCONES

¾ cup unbleached all-purpose flour
½ cup yellow cornmeal
1¼ teaspoons baking powder
1 teaspoon granulated sugar
½ teaspoon salt
pinch of cayenne pepper
3 tablespoons cold unsalted butter, cut into
pieces
¾ cup plus 2 tablespoons coarsely grated
extra-sharp cheddar cheese
1 large egg, separated
⅓ cup milk

These are delicious and light and take about 45 minutes from start to finish. Add more cayenne pepper along with some chopped green onions for more pizzazz.

In a bowl whisk together flour, cornmeal, baking powder, sugar, salt, and cayenne pepper. Cut in the butter until the mixture resembles coarse meal. Stir in ¾ cup of the cheddar. Set aside.

In a small bowl stir together the egg yolk and the milk; add to the flour mixture, and stir with a fork until it just forms a soft dough.

Turn the dough out onto a lightly floured surface, knead it gently 8 to 10 times, and pat it into a 6-inch round. Cut the round with a sharp knife into six equal wedges, arrange the scones about 1 inch apart in a 12″ Dutch oven or on a lightly greased baking sheet, and brush the tops lightly with some of the egg white, beaten lightly. Sprinkle each scone with about 1 teaspoon of the remaining cheddar.

Bake for 15 to 17 minutes, or until they are golden and cooked through. For a conventional oven, bake on the center rack at 400°F for 15 to 17 minutes.

Yield: 6 scones

SWEET POTATO–PECAN MUFFINS

1 medium-sized sweet potato
margarine for greasing muffin tins
½ cup skim milk
½ teaspoon lemon juice
½ cup oats
½ cup shredded wheat bran cereal
⅓ cup dark brown sugar
¼ cup vegetable oil
1 egg
⅔ cup unbleached all-purpose flour
½ teaspoon baking powder
¼ teaspoon baking soda
¼ teaspoon salt
½ teaspoon ground cinnamon
3 teaspoons chopped pecans

These are great low-calorie muffins. Serve with soups or salads.

Bake sweet potato in Dutch oven, conventional oven, or microwave; cool until it can be handled easily. Peel and mash the sweet potato. Set aside ⅓ cup sweet potato; reserve rest for another use.

Grease twelve muffin tins or use paper muffin cups.

In a separate bowl, combine milk, lemon juice, oats, and cereal. Stir well. Add mashed sweet potato, brown sugar, oil, and egg. Beat until smooth and set aside.

In a large bowl, combine flour, baking powder, baking soda, salt, and cinnamon. Make a well in the center of the dry ingredients and pour in oat mixture. Stir just until ingredients are moistened.

Spoon 3 tablespoons batter into each of twelve muffin cups or paper muffin cups inside Dutch oven. Sprinkle each muffin with ¼ teaspoon chopped pecans.

Bake in Dutch oven for 15 minutes, or in 375°F conventional oven for 15 minutes.

Yield: 12 muffins

WHOLE WHEAT BREAD

unsalted butter for greasing pans and rising
    bowl
4 packages active dry yeast
3½ cups warm water
1 cup honey
3 tablespoons oil
1 teaspoon salt
9 cups whole wheat flour
flour for rolling out dough

Liberally butter a bowl and two Dutch ovens; if cooking conventionally, liberally butter a bowl and three loaf pans.

Dissolve yeast in warm water in a large bowl. Add honey and stir until dissolved. Add oil and salt and stir well. Add flour 1 cup at a time, mixing until you have a stiff dough.

Turn dough out onto floured surface and knead until smooth and elastic, about 5 minutes. Shape dough into a ball. Place the dough in oiled bowl and cover with a damp towel or plastic wrap. Let rise until double in size, or about 2 hours.

Cut the dough into two portions for two Dutch ovens or three portions for loaf pans. Shape dough into round or oblong loaves, depending on shape of pans, and place in Dutch ovens or pans. Let rise until double in size.

Bake loaves in Dutch oven for 25 to 30 minutes, or in 350°F conventional oven for about 35 to 40 minutes, until golden brown. Remove from pans immediately and cool slightly before slicing.

Yield: 2 to 3 loaves

OATMEAL BREAD

unsalted butter for greasing pans and rising
   bowl plus 1 tablespoon
¾ cup milk
1 package active dry yeast
1 cup quick oats
1¼ cups boiling water
1½ teaspoons salt
½ cup dark molasses
5 cups unbleached all-purpose flour

This moist bread tastes wonderful and keeps well.

Butter a bowl and two loaf pans or a bowl and two Dutch ovens.

Heat milk over medium heat until a skim forms on the surface. Cool to lukewarm; then stir in yeast. Set aside.

Stir boiling water, salt, and molasses into oats. Cool mixture to lukewarm; then blend in butter, flour, and milk-yeast mixture. Mix until you have a soft dough. Place dough in oiled bowl and cover with a damp towel or plastic wrap. Let dough rise in a warm place until doubled.

Knead lightly about 3 minutes. Shape into two loaves and place in loaf pans or Dutch ovens. Let rise until double again. Bake in Dutch oven for 45 to 50 minutes, or in 350°F for about 1 hour.

Yield: 2 loaves

WHITE CREEK WALNUT BREAD

3 cups plus 2 cups walnuts
1 cup plus 3 cups unbleached
    all-purpose flour
oil for greasing rising bowl
½ cup warm water
1 tablespoon molasses
1 tablespoon active dry yeast
2 cups milk, at room temperature
3 cups whole wheat flour
1½ teaspoon salt
¼ teaspoon nutmeg
1 tablespoon soy sauce
2 tablespoons walnut oil
2 eggs
2 tablespoons milk

Note that some food-processing will need to be done ahead for this recipe.

Do ahead: Grind 3 cups of the walnuts with 1 cup of the all-purpose flour in a blender or food processor until very fine.

Line a 12″ Dutch oven or loaf pan with parchment paper, extending paper 2 inches up sides. Oil bowl for rising.

In a small bowl, combine warm water, molasses, and yeast. Set aside in a warm place until yeast dissolves. Add milk to yeast mixture; then beat in whole wheat flour. Place in oiled bowl and cover with a damp towel or plastic wrap. Let dough rise 1 hour.

Stir dough, and then beat in salt, nutmeg, soy sauce, walnut oil, and one egg.

Add ground walnut–flour mixture to bread dough. Then stir in enough all-purpose flour to make a dough that pulls away from the sides of the bowl. Cover and let sit for 10 minutes.

Knead in the remainder of the all-purpose flour to make a smooth, soft, and slightly sticky dough. Let rise, covered, for 1 hour until dough doubles in size.

While bread is rising, chop the remaining 2 cups of walnuts and toast for 10 minutes in a Dutch oven or in 350°F conventional oven. Beat the remaining egg with 2 tablespoons milk.

Punch down the dough and knead in toasted walnuts. Place in Dutch oven or pan and let rise for about 30 minutes. Glaze loaf with egg-milk mixture.

Bake in Dutch oven for 45 to 55 minutes, or in 375°F conventional oven for 50 to 60 minutes, until loaf is brown and sounds hollow when tapped.

Yield: 1 loaf

PARROT PLACER POPPY-SEED BREAD

6 cups unbleached all-purpose flour
¾ cup whole wheat flour
1 cup rye flour
½ cup poppy seeds
1½ tablespoons sea salt
1 teaspoon fast-acting yeast
2¾ cups warm water
oil for greasing rising bowl
cornmeal for dusting pan
cold water
2 tablespoons poppy seeds

This bread is named for Earl Parrot, a hermit who lived in Impassable Canyon, on the Middle Fork of the Salmon River, from 1917 until 1942. He had a beautiful garden near his cabin, which was only accessible by a 2,000-foot ascent to the canyon rim. In 1990 there remained at the site only the remnants of rhubarb plants, a few fruit trees, and irrigation ditches.

Combine all-purpose flour, wheat flour, rye flour, poppy seeds, sea salt, yeast, and warm water. (If you are doing this at home, you may use a mixer or food processor with a dough-hook attachment.) Knead 10 to 15 minutes if doing by hand and 5 minutes if using a mixer or food processor. Add more warm water if needed, until you have a smooth, elastic dough. Cover with plastic wrap or towel and let rise in oiled bowl or Dutch oven in warm place for the afternoon (or 12 hours in your kitchen).

Dust two Dutch ovens or two loaf pans with cornmeal.

Divide dough in half and form two round loaves. Brush the tops of the loaves with cold water and sprinkle with poppy seeds. Place loaves, poppy-seed-side up, into Dutch ovens or pans. Let the loaves rise until they have doubled in size.

Bake in Dutch oven for 35 to 40 minutes, or in 350°F conventional oven for 45 to 50 minutes, until crusts are golden brown.

Yield: 2 loaves

PARMESAN BREAD

4 packages active dry yeast
4 teaspoons sugar
¼ cup warm water
8 ounces Parmesan cheese, grated (2 cups)
3½ cups plus 3 cups unbleached all-
    purpose flour
2 teaspoons salt
6 eggs, beaten lightly
1½ cups unsalted butter, melted and cooled
oil for coating loaves
unsalted butter for greasing pans

This is a delicious bread to serve with salads.

Dissolve yeast and sugar in warm water. In a separate bowl, mix together Parmesan, 3½ cups of the flour, and salt. Beat in the yeast and eggs; beat mixture for 3 minutes. Add butter and continue beating the mixture, adding the remaining flour as needed to keep the dough from sticking. Knead until a smooth and silky dough is formed. Coat it with oil, cover, and let rise in a covered bowl in a warm place for 2 hours.

Butter three loaf pans or two Dutch ovens.

Cut the dough into two portions for two Dutch ovens or three portions for loaf pans. Shape dough into round or oblong loaves, depending on shape of pans, and place in Dutch ovens or pans. Let rise until double in size.

Bake in Dutch ovens for 25 to 30 minutes, or in 350°F conventional oven for 30 to 35 minutes, until loaves are pale golden and sound hollow when tapped.

Yield: 2 to 3 loaves

SAGE AND OLIVE FOCACCIA BREAD

oil for greasing rising bowl and pan
2 packages active dry yeast
1½ cups lukewarm water
3½ to 4 cups unbleached all-purpose flour
1 cup rye flour
1 tablespoon sage
2 teaspoons rosemary
¼ cup chopped Kalamata olives
2 tablespoons olive oil

Focaccia, a mouth-watering Italian delight, is simpler to make than pizza, because it is usually topped with just a coating of olive oil and a sprinkling of spices and/or herbs. Serve as a snack or a bread.

Grease a 12″ Dutch oven or baking sheet with olive oil. Oil a bowl for rising, and set aside.

Dissolve yeast in water. Add all-purpose flour, rye flour, sage, rosemary, and olives and knead about 5 minutes, gradually working in the rest of the flour. Put dough in oiled bowl, cover with a damp towel or plastic wrap, and let double in size.

Press dough into bottom of Dutch oven or in ½-inch-thick rectangle on baking sheet, cover, and let rise until doubled in size.

Brush top of dough with remaining 2 tablespoons olive oil. Put about ten coals beneath the Dutch oven and a double layer covering the top.

Bake in Dutch oven for 10 minutes, or in 375°F conventional oven for 15 minutes, until brown on top and pulled away from the edges of the pan.

Yield: 1 loaf

THYME-PARMESAN FOCACCIA

5 teaspoons active dry yeast

1 teaspoon sugar

2 cups warm water (105° to 115°F)

1 tablespoon salt

5½ cups unbleached all-purpose flour plus more for rolling out dough

⅓ cup olive oil, plus more for coating dough and pans

2 teaspoons minced fresh thyme leaves (or 1½ teaspoons dried)

2 ounces Parmesan cheese, grated (½ cup)

coarse salt and freshly ground black pepper

Beat together yeast, sugar, and water and let stand 5 minutes, or until foamy. In a bowl, mix salt and 5 cups flour. Set aside. Stir oil into yeast mixture. Gradually add flour mixture to yeast mixture, beating with a heavy spoon or in a standing mixer with dough hook for about 2 minutes until soft and slightly sticky.

Transfer dough to a floured surface and knead in the thyme and enough remaining flour to form a soft but not sticky dough. Form dough into a ball and put in an oiled large bowl, turning to coat. Cover and let rise in a warm place until doubled in bulk, about 45 minutes. For two 12″ Dutch ovens, roll out each half into 12-inch circle and place in Dutch oven to double in size, about 20 minutes. Or oil two 9″ × 13″ baking pans and divide dough in half and roll out to fit pans. Let rise in pans until doubled in size.

Sprinkle dough with Parmesan and salt and pepper. Make indentations, about ½ inch deep and 1 inch apart, all over dough. Bake about 20 minutes. For a conventional oven, bake on center rack at 450°F for 12 minutes, until golden.

Remove focaccia from Dutch ovens or pans and cool.

Yield: 2 loaves

BUBBLE BREAD

oil for greasing rising bowl and pan
(conventional cooking)
2 packages active dry yeast
1 teaspoon sugar
1 cup warm water
1 cup sliced ripe banana
½ cup plus 2 tablespoons pineapple-
orange-banana juice concentrate,
undiluted
¼ cup honey
2 tablespoons margarine, melted
5¼ cups unbleached all-purpose flour
1 teaspoon salt
¼ cup cream of coconut
½ cup confectioners' sugar

Line Dutch oven with parchment paper, extending paper 2 inches up sides. If making in conventional oven, grease a 10" tube pan. Oil a bowl for rising dough.

Dissolve yeast and sugar in warm water and let stand 5 minutes. In a separate bowl, combine banana, ½ cup of juice concentrate, honey, and margarine, and beat well in a blender or by hand until smooth. Set aside.

In a separate large bowl, combine 2 cups of the flour and salt and stir well. Add yeast mixture and banana mixture, stirring until well blended. Add 2¾ more cups of the flour, stirring to form a soft dough. Knead until smooth and elastic, adding remaining flour as needed to prevent dough from sticking to hands. Place in oiled bowl, cover with a damp towel or plastic wrap, and let rise until doubled in size.

Punch down dough and form about thirty 1½-inch balls. Layer balls in Dutch oven or tube pan.

In a small bowl, combine cream of coconut and remaining 2 tablespoons of juice concentrate and stir well. Pour 3 tablespoons of juice mixture over dough. Cover dough and let rise until doubled again.

Bake in Dutch oven for 30 minutes, or in 350°F conventional oven for 30 minutes, until loaf sounds hollow when tapped. Stir confectioners' sugar into remaining juice mixture and drizzle over top of warm bread.

Yield: 1 loaf

SOURDOUGH WHOLE WHEAT BREAD

Sourdough Starter

1 package active dry yeast
½ cup warm water
2 cups lukewarm water
2 cups unbleached all-purpose flour
1 teaspoon salt
1 tablespoon sugar

Bread Dough

1 package active dry yeast
1½ cups warm water
1 cup Sourdough Starter
2 teaspoons salt
2 teaspoons sugar or honey
3 cups plus 2 to 2¼ cups whole wheat flour
½ teaspoon baking soda
flour for rolling out dough
unsalted butter for greasing pans
melted unsalted butter for brushing on
    loaves

Make Sourdough Starter: Dissolve yeast in warm water. Stir in lukewarm water, flour, salt, and sugar. Beat until smooth. Let stand, uncovered at room temperature, for three to five days. Stir two or three times daily; cover at night. (Starter should have a "yeasty," not sour, smell.) Cover, and refrigerate until ready to make bread.

To keep starter: Add ½ cup water, ½ cup flour, and 1 teaspoon sugar to leftover starter. Let stand until bubbly and well fermented, at least one day. Store in the refrigerator or cooler. If not used within ten days, add 1 teaspoon sugar.

Yield: about 3 cups

To make Sourdough Whole Wheat Bread: Soften yeast in warm water in a large bowl. Blend in Sourdough Starter, salt, and sugar or honey. Add 3 cups of the flour. Beat 3 to 4 minutes. Cover with a damp towel or plastic wrap and let rise until double in size (about 2 hours).

In a separate bowl, mix baking soda with 1½ cups of the flour. Stir into risen dough. Add enough additional flour to make a stiff dough. Turn dough out onto a lightly floured surface and knead for 8 to 10 minutes. Divide dough in half, cover, and let rest 10 minutes.

Lightly grease two baking sheets or two Dutch ovens and set aside.

Shape dough into two round or oval loaves. Place loaves on baking sheets or in Dutch ovens. With sharp knife, make diagonal gashes across top. Let rise until double in size (about 1½ hours).

Bake in Dutch oven for 30 to 35 minutes, or in 400°F conventional oven for 35 to 40 minutes. Brush with melted butter.

Yield: 2 loaves

ELVERA'S SOURDOUGH RYE BREAD

1 cup Sourdough Starter (recipe on page 56)
2 cups warm water (about 110°F)
4 cups plus 2½ to 3½ cups unbleached all-
    purpose flour
2 cups rye flour
2 tablespoons light molasses
2 teaspoons salt
1 teaspoon baking soda
1 tablespoon caraway seed
flour for rolling out dough
vegetable shortening for greasing rising bowl
cornmeal for dusting pans
½ cup water
1 teaspoon egg white

My late friend Elvera Klein, author of Creative Sourdough
Recipes, *generously shared some of her wonderful recipes with me.*

Prepare Sourdough Starter and set in a warm place overnight.
The next morning, alternately add the warm water and up to 4
cups of the all-purpose flour to starter. Beat well and set in warm
place for about 3 hours or until bubbly.

Add to starter mixture the rye flour, molasses, salt, baking
soda, caraway seed, and enough all-purpose flour to form a stiff
dough. Turn dough out onto a lightly floured board and knead
until smooth and elastic. Place dough in a greased bowl and turn
dough to grease top as well. Cover with a damp towel or plastic
wrap and let rise in a warm place until doubled in bulk.

Dust a baking sheet or two Dutch ovens with cornmeal. If
making in conventional oven, preheat oven to 400°F.

In a small bowl mix water and egg white. Set aside.

Punch dough down and let rest about 10 minutes. Divide
dough in half and knead each piece gently until smooth. Shape
each piece into an oblong or round loaf. Place on baking sheet or
in Dutch ovens. Set in a warm place to rise until almost double
in size.

If making in conventional oven, just before baking place a
pan with about ¼ inch of boiling water on the lower rack of the
oven.

Cut slashes on top of loaves with a sharp knife or razor blade.
Brush loaves with water–egg white mixture. Bake in Dutch oven
or conventional oven about 25 to 30 minutes or until brown,
brushing with water–egg white mixture again about 10 minutes
before removing bread from oven. Remove from oven or coals
and place on rack to cool.

Yield: 2 loaves

ELVERA'S SOURDOUGH CORN BREAD

unsalted butter for greasing pan plus ¼ cup
    melted
1½ cups yellow cornmeal
½ cup sugar
½ teaspoon salt
¾ teaspoon baking soda
1 cup Sourdough Starter (recipe on page 56)
1½ cups evaporated milk or half and half
2 eggs, beaten

Grease a 12″ Dutch oven or 9″ × 9″ baking pan and set aside.

Mix cornmeal, sugar, salt, and baking soda together in a large bowl and set aside.

In a separate bowl, beat starter, milk, eggs, and butter until just mixed. Stir into cornmeal mixture until well blended.

Pour batter into Dutch oven or baking pan. Bake in Dutch oven or in 400°F oven for 25 to 30 minutes, or until a toothpick inserted in the center comes out clean. Serve hot.

Yield: 1 loaf

AL'S SOURDOUGH BISCUITS

1 cup Sourdough Starter (see recipe on
    page 56)
8 cups unbleached all-purpose flour
1 cup water
½ cup sugar
2½ teaspoons salt
2 tablespoons baking powder
¾ teaspoon baking soda
oil for greasing pan

Al Bukowsky, Solitude River Trips, is an outfitter on the Middle Fork of the Salmon River and a good friend. Famous for his sourdough biscuits, I am flattered that he shared his recipe with me.

The day before, take Sourdough Starter out of cooler or refrigerator and add equal amounts of flour and water (1 cup of each). Let this mixture sit out to warm and expand for 24 hours.

The next day, mix all of the ingredients (except for oil) in a large bowl and stir well.

Add enough Sourdough Starter to make a sticky dough. If needed, add a little water to get the right consistency for your dough.

Roll out dough and pat out large enough area to fill 12″ Dutch oven or your favorite cookie sheet. Cut with a biscuit cutter and place in oiled Dutch oven or on oiled cookie sheet.

Bake for 12 to 15 minutes, until golden brown. For a conventional oven, bake at 350°F for 12 to 15 minutes.

Yield: 10 to 12 servings

COTTAGE CHEESE SOURDOUGH BREAD

1 tablespoon active dry yeast
2 cups lukewarm water
¾ cup Sourdough Starter (recipe on page 56)
1 cup creamed cottage cheese
2 ounces sharp cheddar or Longhorn
    cheese, grated (½ cup)
1 tablespoon chopped fresh dill
2 tablespoons chopped onion
1 tablespoon vegetable oil or melted
    shortening
1 tablespoon sugar
1 tablespoon salt
3 to 4 cups unbleached all-purpose flour
    plus more for rolling out dough
oil or melted shortening for greasing
    rising bowl and pan

Rosemary Parkinson and Peggy Roskelley of Smithfield, Utah, shared their award-winning recipe from the 1988 World Championship Dutch Oven Cookoff. It is held annually in Logan, Utah, as a major event of the Festival of the American West.

Dissolve yeast in water. In a separate large bowl, measure Sourdough Starter and add cottage cheese, cheddar cheese, dill, onion, oil, sugar, and salt. Add dissolved yeast. Gradually beat in enough flour, ½ cup at a time, to make a stiff dough. Reserve ½ cup flour to work into dough during kneading.

Oil a bowl for rising. Grease 14" Dutch oven or large bread pan and set aside.

Turn dough out onto a lightly floured surface and knead for 5 to 10 minutes, adding reserved flour if necessary. Put dough in oiled bowl, turning once to grease top. Cover with a damp cloth or plastic wrap. Set bowl in a warm place and let rise for 2 hours or until doubled in size. It will rise quickly on a warm day. It is wise to have the coals almost ready when the bread is ready to rise.

Place dough in bottom of Dutch oven or pan. Bake in Dutch oven with about twelve coals underneath and eighteen on top for about 35 minutes, or bake in 350°F conventional oven for 35 to 40 minutes.

Yield: 1 large loaf

SHERI'S BREADSTICKS

2½ cups water
1 tablespoon sugar
1 tablespoon salt
1 tablespoon vegetable oil
2 packages active dry yeast
7 to 7¼ cups flour (can use half whole
    wheat and half all-purpose)
unsalted butter for greasing pan plus
    2 tablespoons melted
¼ cup sesame seeds or poppy seeds
seasoned salt or garlic to taste

Sheri Hughes has worked for the Forest Service on the Middle Fork of the Salmon for years. During the summers she was stationed at the launch site in her trailer and prepared these great breadsticks for our guides as a special treat. This dough also makes good pizza crusts.

Heat water, sugar, salt, and oil until warm. Add yeast, making sure the mixture is not hot enough to kill the yeast, and stir. Add flour, and knead resulting dough until smooth and elastic. Let dough rest for 10 minutes.

Lightly grease Dutch oven or baking sheet and set aside.

Roll dough out in long rope and divide into twenty-four shorter pieces. Roll each small piece into desired breadstick shape and place on baking sheet or in Dutch oven. Brush with butter and sprinkle with sesame seeds, poppy seeds, salt, or garlic. Let rise 15 minutes.

Bake in Dutch oven for 15 minutes, or in 400°F conventional oven (on upper rack) for 15 minutes.

Yield: 48 sticks

DUTCH OVEN CINNAMON ROLLS

Whole Wheat Bread Dough

oil for greasing rising bowl plus 3
    tablespoons
4 packages active dry yeast
3½ cups warm water
1 cup honey
1 teaspoon salt
9 cups whole wheat flour

Cinnamon Rolls

flour for rolling out dough
2 tablespoons unsalted butter, melted
1 cup (2 sticks) butter
¼ cup plus ½ cup brown sugar
1 cup raisins
½ cup chopped walnuts
1 teaspoon ground cinnamon

Oil a bowl for rising dough, and set aside.

Dissolve yeast in warm water in a large bowl. Add honey and stir until dissolved. Add oil and salt and stir well. Add flour 1 cup at a time, mixing until you have a stiff dough.

Turn dough out onto floured surface and knead until smooth and elastic, about 5 minutes. Shape dough into a ball. Place the dough in oiled bowl and cover with a damp towel or plastic wrap. Let rise for about 2 hours, until doubled in size.

Divide risen dough in half. On lightly floured board, roll out each half into a ¼-inch-thick rectangle. Brush each rectangle with 1 tablespoon of the melted butter.

Melt the two sticks of butter in the bottom of a 9″ × 12″ baking pan or two Dutch ovens. Sprinkle with ¼ cup brown sugar (⅛ cup in each Dutch oven).

In a separate bowl, combine raisins, ½ cup brown sugar, walnuts, and cinnamon. Sprinkle half of mixture over each piece of dough. Roll up each like a jelly roll, starting with the long edge. Cut rolls into 1-inch slices. Place pieces sealed-side down in pan or Dutch ovens. Cover and let rise until doubled in size, about ½ hour.

Bake in Dutch ovens for about 20 minutes, or in 375°F conventional oven for 25 minutes, until golden brown.

Yield: 30 cinnamon rolls

Salads

Note

During our twenty years of cooking outdoors, we've gathered some great salad and dressing recipes. While most of these don't require a Dutch oven for cooking, they make great accompaniments for Dutch oven meals. Some of the dressings are best made in a food processor, so you'll want to plan ahead before setting out on a camping or river trip. Here's a great way to store and transport premixed dressings: keep dressing in a tightly covered jar in refrigerator or cooler; shake vigorously before serving or tossing with salad ingredients.

POLLY'S CHINESE CHICKEN SALAD

Dressing

6 large garlic cloves, peeled
2 tablespoons chopped, peeled fresh ginger
    root
1½ cups chopped fresh cilantro
1 tablespoon canola oil
1 tablespoon sesame oil
1 tablespoon hot chili oil
½ cup smooth, unsweetened peanut butter
    (natural variety)
½ cup soy sauce
1½ tablespoons sugar
3 tablespoons rice vinegar

Salad

1½ pounds angel hair pasta
3 tablespoons sesame oil
¾ cup chopped fresh cilantro
1½ cups chopped scallions
3 stalks celery, chopped
4 cups chopped, cooked chicken
2 cups cashews, roasted and unsalted

Make the dressing: In a food processor, mince the garlic with ginger root and cilantro; then add canola oil, sesame oil and chili oil, peanut butter, soy sauce, sugar, and vinegar. Blend well. (If you're on the trail or don't have a food processor, you can mince garlic, ginger root, and cilantro together and whisk in other ingredients.) Covered and chilled, the dressing will keep for 1 month.

Make the salad: Cook pasta according to manufacturer's directions and drain. Rinse under cold water until it is cold. Toss pasta with oil, cilantro, scallions, celery, and chicken. The pasta may be prepared up to this point one day in advance if kept covered and chilled.

Just before serving, toss the pasta with the dressing to coat it well, and garnish with cashews.

Yield: 15 servings

SALMON-STUFFED TOMATOES

1 can (16 ounces) pink salmon
3 scallions, chopped
2 stalks celery, chopped
½ cup chopped green olives
2 tablespoons Dijon mustard
¼ cup mayonnaise
1 teaspoon salt-free all-purpose spice mix
6 large, ripe tomatoes
6 lettuce leaves
paprika for garnish

Combine salmon, scallions, celery, olives, mustard, mayonnaise, and spice mix. Mix well and set aside.

Section tomatoes into eighths without cutting all the way through. Spread each tomato open like a flower, and fill with one-sixth of the filling. Place on lettuce leaves and garnish with paprika.

Yield: 6 servings

CURRIED CHICKEN SALAD

4 boneless chicken breasts, skinned
4 tablespoons fresh chopped parsley
1 cup long-grain brown rice
2 cups unsalted chicken broth
2 medium onions, finely chopped
1 tablespoon canola oil
2 stalks celery, finely chopped
3 garlic cloves, finely minced
1 medium tomato, seeded and chopped
1 medium Granny Smith apple
1 tablespoon curry powder
¾ to 1 cup nonfat yogurt
freshly ground pepper to taste
fresh parsley for garnish

This low-fat salad is a meal in itself and makes a perfect dinner for a warm evening.

Poach chicken, cool, and cut into bite-sized pieces. Combine with parsley and set aside. Cook rice in chicken broth.

Sauté onions in oil until tender. Add celery and cook 5 minutes longer. Mix in garlic and tomato. Cook 5 more minutes and remove from heat.

Core apple and cut into ¼-inch cubes. Add to vegetable mixture. Blend in curry powder and mix well. Add rice and vegetable mixture to chicken. Add yogurt and mix just until blended.

Adjust seasonings to taste. Sprinkle ground pepper and parsley on top. Serve at room temperature or chill before serving.

Yield: 6 servings

SHRIMP AND CABBAGE SALAD

Dressing
1 envelope Hidden Valley Ranch dressing
1 cup whole milk
1 cup mayonnaise
1 avocado, peeled and mashed

Salad
½ head green cabbage, chopped
½ head red cabbage, chopped
2 cans (6 ounces each) medium or large
    shrimp, drained

Make the dressing: Mix Hidden Valley Ranch dressing with milk and mayonnaise according to package directions. Combine with mashed avocado and set aside.

Make the salad: Combine green cabbage, red cabbage, and shrimp. Pour dressing over salad and toss.

Yield: 6 to 8 servings

TORTELLINI SALAD

1 cup chopped walnuts
2 packages (9 ounces each) fresh meat- or
    cheese-filled tortellini pasta, cooked and
    chilled
½ cup chopped scallions
½ red bell pepper, chopped
1 large tomato, chopped
2 stalks celery, chopped
pepper to taste
salt-free spice mix to taste
1 cup Dijon-type vinaigrette

Toast walnuts for 10 minutes in Dutch oven, or for 10 minutes in 350°F conventional oven. Combine with rest of ingredients and toss. Chill before serving.

Yield: 6 servings

BLACK BEAN SALAD

2 cups dried black beans
3½ cups water
1 cup chopped scallions
3 garlic cloves, crushed
1 large carrot, chopped
2 tomatoes, chopped
1 cup chopped cilantro
1½ teaspoons cumin
1 teaspoon cayenne pepper
1 jar (12–16 ounces) salsa
lettuce for salad beds
yogurt and chips for garnish

Rinse black beans, put in a Dutch oven or large saucepan, and cover with water. Soak them several hours or overnight.

Pour off excess water, leaving enough to cover beans, and simmer beans 1½ hours over low heat. Drain and chill.

Toss beans with scallions, garlic, carrot, tomatoes, cilantro, cumin, cayenne pepper, and salsa. Serve on a bed of fresh lettuce with a dollop of yogurt on top and tortilla chips on the side. This salad is also delicious stuffed into red bell peppers or tomatoes.

Yield: 6 servings

JALAPEÑO POTATO SALAD

Dressing
4 tablespoons Dijon mustard
¼ cup wine vinegar
½ cup olive oil
2 garlic cloves, minced
salt and black pepper to taste

Salad
4 medium russet potatoes (unpeeled),
    cooked and cubed
1 can medium, pitted black olives, chopped
6 jalapeño peppers, seeded and sliced
1 cup chopped scallions
6 ounces feta cheese, crumbled

Mix dressing ingredients in a small bowl.

In a large bowl, combine potatoes, olives, peppers, scallions, and cheese. Pour dressing over all and toss. Adjust seasoning to taste.

Yield: 6 servings

POVERTY FLAT POTATO SALAD

4 medium-sized potatoes (unpeeled),
   cooked and cubed
1 red onion, chopped
3 stalks celery, chopped
½ cup chopped dill pickles
½ cup chopped green pepper
3 eggs, hard-cooked and cubed
½ cup mayonnaise
3 tablespoons Dijon mustard
1 teaspoon fresh ground pepper

Around 1900, Joe Groff worked a mining claim near the Main Salmon River. It had an open area known as Poverty Flat, where nothing would grow. This simple salad is named for the area.

Combine all ingredients and chill.

Yield: 6 to 8 servings

WILD RICE SALAD

Salad
1 cup uncooked wild rice
2 cups chicken broth
1 cup snow peas, cut in bite-sized pieces
6 scallions, chopped
½ cup chopped red bell pepper
¼ cup sliced water chestnuts
½ cup sliced mushrooms
1 can black olives, sliced in half

Dressing
⅓ cup tarragon vinegar
1 teaspoon salt (optional)
1 teaspoon dried tarragon leaves
¼ cup safflower oil or olive oil

My sister-in-law, Betty Mills, uses wild rice grown by her friends in St. Maries, Idaho, to complement the nutty flavor of this salad. Rice can be cooked ahead of time and stored in a cooler or refrigerator.

Boil rice in chicken broth for 10 minutes and reduce to simmer for 40 minutes or until rice is rather nutty in texture. Drain and cool.

Add peas, scallions, bell pepper, water chestnuts, mushrooms, and black olives. Stir and set aside.

In a small bowl, combine dressing ingredients. Pour over salad and toss. Chill before serving.

Yield: 6 servings

BROCCOLI WITH DIJON VINAIGRETTE

2 pounds fresh broccoli florets
4 teaspoons olive oil
¼ cup finely chopped scallions
½ teaspoon dried tarragon
½ teaspoon dry mustard
3 garlic cloves, minced
2 tablespoons balsamic vinegar
2 tablespoons water
1 tablespoon Dijon mustard
¼ teaspoon ground black pepper
⅛ teaspoon salt

Steam broccoli for 6 minutes or until crisp-tender. Drain and put into a bowl. Heat olive oil in skillet and sauté scallions, tarragon, dry mustard, and garlic for 3 minutes.

Remove from heat and add vinegar, water, Dijon mustard, pepper, and salt, stirring until blended. Drizzle over broccoli, tossing to coat. Serve while warm.

Yield: 8 servings

BLUE CHEESE WALNUT SALAD

1 cup broken walnut pieces
1 bunch leaf lettuce
1 Granny Smith apple, chopped
4 ounces blue cheese, crumbled (1 cup)
1 cup Dijon-type vinaigrette

Toast walnuts for 10 minutes in Dutch oven, or for 10 minutes in 350°F conventional oven. Tear the lettuce into pieces and toss with walnuts and remaining ingredients.

Yield: 6 servings

HEARTS OF PALM AND RED PEPPER SALAD

1 bunch leaf lettuce
1 can (12–14 ounces) hearts of palm,
    sliced into ½-inch pieces
1 red bell pepper, seeded and sliced in strips
1 jar capers, drained
½ cup Dijon-type vinaigrette
freshly ground black pepper to taste

Tear the lettuce into pieces and toss with palm, pepper, capers, and vinaigrette. Top with pepper to taste.

Yield: 6 servings

BIG CREEK BROCCOLI SALAD

Salad
½ head cauliflower, cut into
    small florets
½ head broccoli, cut into small florets
2 medium-sized tomatoes, cut into chunks
1 small red onion, chopped
1 can black olives, drained and chopped
½ cup sunflower seeds
1 cup peas (frozen or fresh), blanched and
    chilled

Dressing
¼ cup wine vinegar
¼ cup olive oil
⅛ teaspoon mustard seed
⅛ teaspoon celery seed
1 teaspoon sweet basil
salt and black pepper to taste

My good friend Catherine Scott, a home designer in Boise, shared this great recipe with me. Big Creek is a major tributary in Impassable Canyon on the Middle Fork of the Salmon River.

Combine vegetables and sunflower seeds. In a separate bowl, combine dressing ingredients. Pour over vegetables and toss. Chill before serving.

Yield: 6 to 8 servings

ORANGE PECAN SALAD

1 cup pecan pieces
1 can (8 ounces) mandarin oranges, or 2
    fresh oranges, peeled and sectioned
1 bunch leaf lettuce
½ red onion, thinly sliced
1 bunch radishes, thinly sliced

This is great served with Sheila's Honey Mustard Dressing.

Toast pecans for 10 minutes in Dutch oven or for 10 minutes in 350°F conventional oven. Toss with remaining ingredients. Chill before serving.

Yield: 6 servings

SHEILA'S HONEY MUSTARD DRESSING

3 tablespoons plus 1 teaspoon Dijon
    mustard
7 tablespoons honey
½ cup apple cider vinegar
1 cup oil (canola or olive)

Mix all ingredients very well.

Yield: Slightly less than 1 cup

SPICY BUTTERMILK DRESSING

1 cup buttermilk
1 tablespoon Dijon-style mustard
1 tablespoon minced onion
¼ teaspoon dried dill weed
1 tablespoon chopped fresh parsley
⅛ teaspoon salt
⅛ teaspoon black pepper

Combine all ingredients in a jar, cover, and shake to blend. Adjust spices to taste. Chill. Shake well again before using.

Yield: 1 cup

GREEN'S SALAD DRESSING FOR GREENS

1 egg
2 ounces Parmesan cheese, grated (½ cup)
¼ cup lemon juice
2 garlic cloves, minced
1 teaspoon Worcestershire sauce
½ teaspoon black pepper
½ cup olive oil

My friend Melissa Green prepares this great dressing in advance for river trips.

Blend egg, Parmesan, lemon juice, garlic, Worcestershire, and pepper at low speed. Add olive oil and blend again. Chill 1 hour before serving.

Yield: about 1 cup

ARTICHOKE PASTA SALAD

4 ounces cooked tricolor rotini (corkscrew)
   pasta
1 6-ounce jar marinated artichoke hearts,
   drained
¼ pound fresh white button mushrooms,
   quartered
1 cup cherry tomatoes, halved
1 cup medium-sized pitted ripe olives
1 tablespoon chopped fresh Italian parsley
½ teaspoon dry basil leaves (or 1 teaspoon
   chopped fresh)
salt and black pepper to taste
¼ cup vinaigrette

*This is a colorful, tasty vegetable salad and quick and easy
to prepare. Use the marinade from the artichoke hearts as a
dressing, your favorite vinaigrette or Newman's Own Caesar's
Dressing to taste.*

Combine all of the above ingredients and toss well. Cover and
chill for at least 4 hours.

Yield: 6 servings

BECKY'S CALL SALAD

½ bunch of leaf lettuce
½ cup dried cranberries
¼ cup gorgonzola crumbles
¼ cup roasted, broken pecans
your favorite vinaigrette, if desired

*While doing their residencies at Dartmouth, Mark and Becky
Uranga created this salad to pack into Becky's lunch bag for
lunch or dinner the nights she is on call. It combines all of Becky's
favorite salad ingredients which are hardy so it can be made in
the morning, stored in the refrigerator and eaten without dressing
after a quick toss.*

Combine lettuce, cranberries, gorgonzola, and pecans. Toss with
vinaigrette if desired.

Yield: 2 servings

ENTSALADA MIXTA

½ bunch leaf lettuce, torn
2 medium cooked potatoes, cut into chunks
3 medium tomatoes, thinly sliced
3 hard-boiled eggs, sliced
4 ounces albacore tuna in olive oil, broken
    with a fork
1 jar white asparagus
salt to taste
white wine vinegar
extra-virgin olive oil

This salad from Mark Uranga is best in the summertime with fresh tomatoes from his Dad, Louis's, garden in Boise, Idaho. Mark and Becky make a point to of sharing it with Basque friends. And, for almost every one of them, it takes them all back to a table in the Basque Country and just the start of another unbelievable meal.

Combine lettuce, potatoes, tomatoes, eggs, tuna, and asparagus. Toss with salt, vinegar and olive oil and serve.

Yield: 4 servings

CHICKEN AND CABBAGE ASIAN SALAD

¼ cup slivered almonds, toasted
¾ tablespoons sesame seeds, toasted
1 package Asian-flavored Ramen noodles
8 ounces cooked, shredded chicken
1¼ pounds cabbage, shredded
¼ pound carrots, shredded
1 bunch scallions with tops, chopped
2 tablespoons sugar
⅛ cup rice vinegar
2 tablespoons sesame oil
1 tablespoon chili oil
¼ cup olive oil
½ teaspoon salt
½ teaspoon freshly ground pepper

Roast almonds, sesame seeds, and broken Ramen noodles until golden. Combine chicken, cabbage, carrots, scallions, roasted almond mix and mix well.

Chill. Combine Ramen seasoning, sugar, vinegar, oils, salt, and pepper in jar. Chill and toss with salad.

Yield: 6 to 8 servings

GRILLED BLACKBERRY CHICKEN SALAD

½ cup raspberry or balsamic vinegar
¼ cup blackberry jam
2 tablespoons Dijon mustard
1 teaspoon sugar
4 4-ounce boneless, skinless chicken
  breasts
4 ounces mixed baby greens
1 pint blackberries
1½ ounces crumbled mild goat cheese,
  such as Montrachet
½ cup snipped fresh chives
salt and freshly ground pepper to taste

A favorite of Allison Lawrence of Boise, Idaho, my cousin and former river guide.

Combine vinegar, jam, mustard, and sugar. Blend with a fork until smooth. Pour half of the dressing over chicken in shallow dish. Turn the chicken to coat evenly. Refrigerate for at least 10 minutes, or up to one hour.

Coat grill with oil. Grill the chicken for 6 minutes on each side. Transfer to a cutting surface and let stand for 5 minutes before cutting crosswise into thin slices.

Mix greens with reserved dressing and divide among four plates. Sprinkle evenly with berries. Top with chicken slices. Garnish with goat cheese and chives, dividing evenly. Season with salt and pepper.

Yield: 4 servings

JICAMA SLAW

1 large jicama, peeled and shredded
2 15-ounce cans black beans, rinsed and
  drained
3–4 large carrots, peeled and shredded
2 mangos, peeled and chunked
1 large avocado, chunked
1 large jalapeño, seeded and diced
½ cup chopped cilantro,
juice of 1 lime
6 flour tortillas

Great salad for camping from Allison Lawrence.

Combine jicama, beans, carrots, mangos, avocado, jalapeño, and cilantro. Stir gently. Add lime juice. Divide slaw among tortillas and serve.

Yield: 6 servings

HEARTY POTATO SALAD

Salad
6–8 medium red potatoes, boiled, cooled,
    and sliced
1 large red onion, sliced into rings

Vinaigrette
¼ cup chicken stock
½ cup olive oil
¼ cup white wine vinegar
1 teaspoon dried tarragon
1 tablespoon finely chopped parsley
1 teaspoon salt

Mary Jo Mulick, a great friend from Pocatello, Idaho, found this easy salad recipe in the Idaho State Journal years ago.

Combine potatoes and onions. Set aside. Combine vinaigrette ingredients and then pour over salad. Mix and serve at room temperature.

Yield: 6 servings

CORN AND BLACK BEAN SALAD

Salad
2 cups fresh or frozen corn kernels
1 15-ounce can black beans, washed and
    drained
1 large tomato, chopped
¼ red onion, chopped
1 avocado, chopped
½ cup chopped cilantro

Dressing
¼ cup cider vinegar
2 teaspoons sugar
¼ teaspoon cumin

This salad goes well with the Creamy Chicken Enchiladas.

Combine salad ingredients. Toss with dressing and chill.

Yield: 6 servings

SPICY PEANUT BUTTER LINGUINI SALAD

Dressing

¼ cup soy sauce
1½ tablespoons sugar
1 tablespoon sesame oil
1 tablespoon ground ginger
¼ teaspoon cayenne pepper
½ tablespoon minced garlic
¼ cup rice vinegar
¾ cup creamy peanut butter
¼ cup chicken broth

Salad

8 ounces linguini
1 cup shredded, cooked chicken, chilled
1 orange or yellow bell pepper, chopped
½ cup chopped green onions
¼ cup shredded carrots
¼ cup chopped cilantro
freshly ground black pepper to taste
¼ cup salted, roasted peanuts

Make the dressing: Whisk together dressing ingredients and set aside.

Make the salad: Cook pasta according to package directions until al dente. Drain and rinse. Add chicken, bell pepper, green onions, carrots, and cilantro. Add dressing and toss until coated. Season with pepper. Chill for an hour. Add peanuts right before serving.

Yield: 6 to 8 servings

TOMATO AND CUCUMBER SUMMER SALAD

⅓ cup extra-virgin olive oil
¼ cup fresh lemon juice
1 tablespoon white vinegar
1¼ teaspoons salt
1 teaspoon ground cumin
½ teaspoon black pepper
4 cups vine-ripened diced tomatoes
2½ cups seedless diced cucumber
1 bunch fresh parsley, chopped
¼ cup finely chopped sweet onion

Whisk together oil, lemon juice, vinegar, salt, cumin, and pepper. Add tomatoes, cucumber, parsley, and onion and stir. Let stand at room temperature 15 minutes before serving.

Yield: 4 to 6 servings

VERMONTER SALAD

Salad
½ bunch leaf lettuce, torn in pieces
½ pint fresh blueberries
¼ cup crumbled feta cheese
¼ cup roasted pine nuts

Dressing
white wine vinegar
extra-virgin olive oil
salt and freshly ground black pepper to taste

Our guide, Mark Uranga, is doing his residency at Dartmouth and sent me this recipe with the following comment. "Even though I was making this salad before we moved here to northern New England, it was here this salad really began to make sense. Most of these ingredients can be found locally in the midsummer when the blueberries ripen." You can use Maple Balsamic Dressing from Stonewood Kitchens if you like.

Combine lettuce, blueberries, cheese, and pine nuts. Combine dressing ingredients and toss with salad.

Yield: 2 servings

Appetizers, Snacks, and Sandwiches

Remember

When a recipe calls for baking, braising, stewing, or roasting, the Dutch oven must be covered with charcoal briquettes on top of the lid. For boiling, frying, sautéing, and quick heating, leave the Dutch oven cover off. For more on cooking techniques for the Dutch oven, see "Dutch Oven Care and Use," pages 2–4. When using a conventional oven, preheat the oven to the given baking temperature.

BASIL PESTO DIP

5 garlic cloves
¾ cup firmly packed fresh basil leaves
3 tablespoons almonds, blanched
3 tablespoons olive oil
3 ounces Parmesan cheese, grated (¾ cup)
24 ounces whole-milk ricotta cheese, at
    room temperature

Place the garlic, basil, and almonds in the bowl of a food processor or blender. With the motor running, slowly drizzle in the oil through the feed tube. Process until the basil is pureed. Transfer the pesto to a bowl and stir in the Parmesan cheese. (The pesto can be refrigerated for up to three days.)

To complete the dip, beat ricotta and pesto in a mixer or food processor until well blended. Cover and chill until ready to use. Serve on crackers, toasted French bread, or stuffed into cherry tomatoes.

Yield: 4 cups

PAPAYA SALSA

3 medium-sized cucumbers, peeled and
    diced
3 fresh jalapeño peppers, seeded and
    minced
1 medium-sized onion, minced
3 papayas, peeled and cubed
2 mangos, peeled and cubed (as best you
    can)
2 cans (20 ounces each) crushed or diced
    pineapple, drained
½ cup fresh lime juice
1 red bell pepper, chopped
3 kiwis, peeled and chopped

This salsa is great served with grilled fish or pork, or any dish you want to give a tropical flavor.

Combine all ingredients, cover, and chill.

Yield: 7 to 8 cups

CHILI-CHEESE DIP

2 pounds Velveeta cheese, cubed
4 cans (14–16 ounces each) chili without
   beans
2 cans (7 ounces each) chopped green
   chiles

Mix all ingredients then heat slowly in Dutch oven, saucepan, or microwave until melted. Stir again. Serve warm with tortilla chips.

Yield: about 8 cups

CRAB-STUFFED MUSHROOMS

12 large mushrooms
2 tablespoons minced scallions (use green
   part)
2 tablespoons plus 3 tablespoons unsalted
   butter
1 teaspoon lemon juice
1 cup flaked, cooked crab meat
½ cup wheat germ
½ cup sour cream
3 ounces Swiss cheese, grated (¾ cup)
¼ cup chicken broth
lemon wedges for garnish

Wipe mushrooms with a damp cloth. Remove and finely chop the stems. Sauté mushroom stems and scallions in 2 tablespoons of the butter until onion is limp. Remove from heat and stir in lemon juice, crab meat, wheat germ, sour cream, and a third of the cheese.

Melt remaining 3 tablespoons butter in Dutch oven or 9″ × 12″ baking dish. Turn mushroom caps in the butter until well coated. Spoon about 2 tablespoons of the crab-meat mixture into each cap. Place mushrooms, filled-side up, in Dutch oven or dish.

Before baking, sprinkle mushrooms with the remaining cheese and pour broth around mushrooms in bottom of Dutch oven or dish.

Bake in Dutch oven for 10 to 15 minutes, or in 350°F conventional oven for 15 to 20 minutes. Serve hot with lemon wedges.

Yield: 6 servings

BRUSCHETTA WITH SUMMER TOMATOES

2 garlic cloves, finely chopped
3 ripe red tomatoes, coarsely chopped and
    drained
¼ cup chopped fresh basil
¼ cup chopped fresh parsley
⅓ cup olive oil
½ teaspoon salt
½ teaspoon freshly ground black pepper
8 thick slices crusty Italian or French bread

This traditional grilled Italian treat tastes great made with vine-ripe tomatoes.

Combine all ingredients except bread and set aside.

Grill bread slices on both sides in skillet, on Dutch oven lid, or in bottom of Dutch oven until crisp. Top with tomato mixture and serve immediately.

Yield: 8 servings

GREEN SALSA

2 fresh jalapeño peppers, seeded
4 to 6 fresh Anaheim peppers, seeded
6 green peppers, seeded
4 garlic cloves, peeled
2 avocados, peeled and pitted
2 tablespoons chopped cilantro
1 tablespoon olive oil
dash fresh lime juice

Karen Culbertson, a river guide and ski patroller, gave me this great salsa recipe. Prepare this ahead of time at home before you go camping or on a river trip.

Blend all ingredients in a blender until smooth. Serve with tortilla chips.

Yield: about 2 cups

NOT-FOR-THE-FAINTHEARTED NACHOS

2 large heads of garlic, separated into
    cloves and peeled
2 tablespoons olive oil
1 package (10 ounces) tortilla chips
¼ cup chopped red onion
1 can (4 ounces) green chiles, chopped
⅓ cup pimiento-stuffed green olives, sliced
6 ounces Monterey Jack cheese, grated
    (1½ cups)
chopped cilantro and chopped scallions for
    garnish

Coat garlic cloves with olive oil, cover, and bake in Dutch oven for 30 minutes, or in 350°F conventional oven for 30 minutes, or until soft and golden.

Cover the bottom of 12″ Dutch oven or 9″ × 12″ baking pan with tortilla chips.

Mash the garlic, and mix in onion, chiles, and olives. Spread evenly over chips and cover with cheese. Bake in Dutch oven or in 375°F conventional oven for 5 minutes, or until cheese melts. Top with cilantro and scallions.

Yield: 6 servings

MUSHROOMS AU GRATIN

1 pound fresh mushrooms
2 tablespoons unsalted butter
⅓ cup sour cream
¼ teaspoon salt
dash black pepper
1 tablespoon unbleached all-purpose flour
¼ cup chopped fresh parsley
2 ounces Swiss or mild cheddar cheese,
    grated (½ cup)

Slice mushrooms lengthwise in ¼-inch pieces. Heat butter in skillet or Dutch oven over medium heat; sauté mushrooms. Cover pan for about 2 minutes, until the mushrooms begin to exude juices.

In a separate bowl, blend sour cream, salt, pepper, and flour until smooth. Stir into mushroom mixture in pan and heat, stirring, until blended and beginning to boil.

Sprinkle parsley and cheese over mixture and heat until cheese melts, about 10 minutes. Serve with crackers or toasted French bread.

Yield: 4 servings

CHEDDAR BISCUITS WITH HAM

1¾ cups unbleached all-purpose flour
2 teaspoons baking powder
1 teaspoon salt
3 tablespoons unsalted butter
2 ounces cheddar cheese, grated (½ cup)
¾ cup buttermilk
½ cup chopped green scallions
½ cup (1 stick) butter
½ pound Black Forest ham or any good-
    quality ham, thinly sliced

These biscuits make a delicious appetizer. Serve them hot out of the oven.

Line two Dutch ovens or a baking sheet with parchment paper.

In a large bowl, combine flour, baking powder, and salt. Add butter and blend with a pastry blender or your fingers until mixture resembles coarse meal. Stir in cheese. Add buttermilk and scallions and mix well.

Roll out dough to ½-inch thickness. Cut out biscuits using 1½-inch round cutter. Gather scraps, reroll, and cut again, using all of the dough. Place biscuits on parchment paper (they should not touch each other).

Bake in Dutch oven or in 350°F conventional oven for about 15 minutes, or until biscuits are puffed and light golden. Cool.

Split and lightly butter biscuits. Stuff with ham slices. Return biscuits to Dutch ovens or conventional oven and bake 5 minutes or until heated through.

Yield: about 35 biscuits

OLIVADA

1 cup pimento-stuffed green olives
1 cup Kalamata olives, pitted
1 cup black olives, pitted
1 tablespoon capers
1 tablespoon olive oil
½ cup tomatillo salsa

Blend all ingredients in food processor. Refrigerate. Serve on French bread or crackers, or use as a sandwich spread.

Yield: 3 cups

ASPARAGUS AND CHEESE SANDWICHES

4 whole wheat English muffins, halved
1 package (10 ounces) frozen asparagus
    spears, thawed and drained
1 can (12–14 ounces) pitted black olives,
    sliced
16 ounces Swiss cheese, sliced or grated
    (4 cups)
Jiffy Hollandaise (see recipe below) or 1
    package instant hollandaise sauce
paprika for garnish

Toast muffins in Dutch oven or under broiler. Arrange asparagus, olives, and cheese on muffins. Bake in Dutch oven with briquettes on top and underneath or put under broiler in conventional oven until cheese melts.

Prepare Hollandaise sauce, drizzle sauce over each muffin half, and sprinkle with paprika.

Yield: 6 to 8 servings

JIFFY HOLLANDAISE

¼ cup sour cream
¼ cup mayonnaise
½ teaspoon mustard
1 teaspoon lemon juice

Combine all ingredients. Cook and stir over low heat until heated through.

Yield: ½ cup

GRILLED CHEESE-AND-AVOCADO SANDWICHES

8 slices whole wheat bread
4 tablespoons unsalted butter
4 large slices cheddar cheese
2 ripe avocados, sliced
3 ounces cream cheese, softened

Butter both sides of bread. Layer cheese, avocados, and cream cheese on one slice of bread and top with another slice.

Grill in skillet, on Dutch oven lid, or in bottom of Dutch oven until bread is golden brown and cheese is melted. Cut sandwiches in half and serve.

Yield: 4 servings

GRILLED CREAM-CHEESE-AND-OLIVE SANDWICHES

8 slices whole wheat bread
4 tablespoons unsalted butter
8 ounces cream cheese, softened
1 can (10–12 ounces) pitted black olives, sliced

Butter both sides of bread. Spread cream cheese generously on four slices of bread. Sprinkle olive slices over cream cheese. Top with another slice of bread.

Grill in skillet, on Dutch oven lid, or in bottom of Dutch oven until bread is golden brown and cheese is soft. Cut sandwiches in half and serve.

Yield: 4 servings

CRACKER BREAD SANDWICHES

3 rounds Middle Eastern cracker bread
  (14-inch diameter)
10 ounces cream cheese, softened
1 package (6 ounces) alfalfa sprouts
4 ripe tomatoes, thinly sliced
4 avocados, peeled, pitted, and thinly sliced
2 medium-sized cucumbers, thinly sliced
12 ounces cheddar cheese, grated (3 cups)
1 can (12–14 ounces) black olives, chopped

Serve this as an appetizer or for lunch.

Follow package directions for preparing cracker bread.

   Spread one layer of cracker bread with cream cheese; then layer the sprouts and tomatoes. Place another cracker on top and layer with avocados, cucumbers, cheddar cheese, and olives. Top with third cracker and cut into squares or wedges.

Yield: 10 to 12 servings

CLIFFSIDE CRAB SALAD SANDWICHES

1 pound fresh or canned crab, chopped
⅓ cup mayonnaise
1 cup diced celery
1 teaspoon seafood seasoning
freshly ground pepper
⅓ cup diced sweet onion
1 loaf sliced wheat bread or 1 package
  bagels
1 cup wasabi mayonnaise (can be
  purchased in a specialty grocery store)
  or plain, if preferred
1 bunch green leaf lettuce

Blend together crab, mayonnaise, celery, seafood seasoning, pepper, and onions. Spread bread with wasabi or plain mayonnaise and top with crab mixture and lettuce leaves and top with another slice of bread.

Yield: 6 servings

ASPARAGUS PASTRY ROLLS

1 frozen puff pastry sheet, thawed
¼ cup flour
1 large egg yolk, lightly beaten
1 tablespoon cold water
1 cup packed finely grated Parmesan
    cheese
½ pound prosciutto, sliced thinly and cut
    into 6-inch strips
14 ¾-inch asparagus stalks trimmed to
    6-inch lengths
2 tablespoons white truffle oil

Unfold pastry sheet and cut in half parallel to fold lines. Roll out half into a 20″ × 7″ rectangle a on a well-floured surface. Brush off excess flour from work surface and both sides of pastry, trim edges to make even. Cut crosswise into 6 (6½ by 3-inch) rectangles.

Combine egg yolk and water. Brush rectangles with some egg wash and sprinkle each evenly with 1 packed tablespoon cheese, leaving a ½-inch border on long sides. Lay a piece of prosciutto and a stalk or asparagus along one long side, then roll up in pastry, pressing seam to seal. Continue with the rest of the asparagus.

Arrange rolls, seam sides down, about 1 inch apart in a 12″ Dutch oven and brush with remaining egg wash. Chill rolls until pastry is firm, at least 15 minutes. Bake for about 15 minutes. For a conventional oven, bake at 400°F for 15 minutes or until puffed and golden. Cut each roll into 4 pieces and drizzle with truffle oil. Serve warm.

Yield: 10 to 12 servings

SUN-DRIED TOMATO AND GARLIC DIP

1 cup sun-dried tomatoes in oil
4 cloves garlic, crushed
¼ cup chopped fresh basil
8 ounces cream cheese
sour cream

Chop tomatoes in food processor. Add garlic, oil from sun-dried tomatoes, basil, and cream cheese. Add sour cream and process until smooth consistency for a dip. Serve with crackers.

Yield: 8 servings

FIRE ISLAND BEAN DIP

1 teaspoon vegetable oil
½ cup chopped onion
2 garlic cloves, minced
½ cup diced tomato
⅓ cup bottled picante sauce
½ teaspoon chili powder
½ teaspoon ground cumin
1 15-ounce can black beans, rinsed and
   drained
¼ cup shredded Monterey Jack cheese
¼ cup chopped fresh cilantro
1 tablespoon fresh lime juice

Jeana and Al Bukowsky shared this great starter that they serve on their Solitude River Trips on the Middle Fork of the Salmon.

Heat oil in a 12″ Dutch oven or medium-sized skillet over medium heat. Add onion and garlic and sauté 4 minutes or until soft. Add tomato, picante sauce, chili powder, cumin and black beans; cook 5 minutes or until thick, stirring constantly. Remove from heat; partially mash with a potato masher. Add cheese, cilantro, and lime juice, stirring until cheese melts. Serve warm or at room temperature with tortilla chips.

Yield: 1⅔cups

Poultry and Fish Dishes

Remember

When a recipe calls for baking, braising, stewing, or roasting, the Dutch oven must be covered with charcoal briquettes on top of the lid. For boiling, frying, sautéing, and quick heating, leave the Dutch oven cover off. For more on cooking techniques for the Dutch oven, see "Dutch Oven Care and Use," pages 2–4. When using a conventional oven, preheat the oven at the given baking temperature.

CHICKEN CACCIATORE

6 garlic cloves, sliced
1 large onion, sliced
1½ teaspoons dried oregano leaves
1½ teaspoons chopped fresh sweet basil
1 teaspoon chopped fresh parsley
1 teaspoon anise seeds
1 cup fresh mushrooms, cut in half
3 tablespoons plus 1 tablespoon olive oil
1 large cut-up chicken (or equivalent
    quantity of venison, pheasant, duck,
    or rabbit)
3 cans (6 ounces each) tomato paste
5 cans (8 ounces each) tomato sauce
1 cup water
1 can (6 ounces) pitted black olives, drained
2 tablespoons sugar
½ teaspoon salt
½ teaspoon black pepper
2 tablespoons grated Parmesan cheese
5 whole bay leaves

This is a family recipe from Cornellia Caccia, a Pocatello chef responsible for the success of several Italian restaurants in south-eastern Idaho. Cornellia's nephew, John Caccia, likes to prepare and freeze this dish in advance. He also suggests expanding your horizons by substituting venison, pheasant, duck, or rabbit for the classic chicken.

In a large Dutch oven, sauté garlic, onion, oregano leaves, basil, parsley, anise seeds, and mushrooms in 3 tablespoons of the olive oil. Set aside.

In a frying pan, brown chicken in remaining tablespoon of oil. In a separate bowl, mix tomato paste, tomato sauce, water, olives, sugar, salt, pepper, Parmesan, and bay leaves. Add the browned chicken and tomato sauce mixture to the Dutch oven. Simmer for 3 hours. Remove bay leaves.

When properly cooked, the chicken meat will just fall off the bones. Serve over noodles or cornbread. You can use any leftover sauce to make pizza.

Yield: 6 servings

Variations: *A great vegetarian adaptation to this hunter-style Italian dish was given to me by John's brother, Bill Caccia, a longtime friend. Refer to page 142 for Tofu Cacciatore recipe.*

SAUCY CHICKEN

6 chicken breasts, skinned, trimmed of
    excess fat, split, and halved
2 tablespoons olive oil
1 large onion, chopped
2 medium shallots, minced
2 tablespoons unsalted butter
12 ounces fresh mushrooms, sliced
2 tablespoons unbleached all-purpose flour
2⅓ cups chicken stock or canned low-
    sodium broth
½ cup low-fat sour cream
salt and black pepper to taste
2 jars (4 ounces each) pimientos, drained
    and diced
2 tablespoons minced cilantro

This dish is wonderful served warm with corn bread on the side. For a unique sandwich, pile the chicken mixture between two slices of corn bread.

Brown chicken in oil until partially cooked. Set aside. Cook onion and shallots in butter until softened and slightly browned. Add mushrooms and cook for 6 to 8 minutes. Stir in flour and cook for an additional 5 minutes. Add ⅓ cup chicken broth and cook until the mixture becomes thick and pasty.

Gradually add the rest of the stock or broth, stirring until stock is thickened slightly. Stir in sour cream and adjust seasoning with salt and pepper to taste. Stir in pimientos and cilantro.

Cut the chicken off the bones, add to sauce, and let cook about 5 minutes or until chicken is cooked through.

Yield: 6 to 8 servings

CHICKEN CURRY

¼ cup olive oil
¼ cup red curry paste (available at Asian
    markets)
2 teaspoons curry powder
6 tablespoons fermented fish sauce
    (available at Asian markets)
1 chicken breast, boned and sliced
2 potatoes, peeled and cut into 16 to 20
    slices
2 carrots, cut into 16 to 20 slices
4 cups coconut milk

Heat the oil and add curry paste and curry powder. Stir-fry over high heat for 1 minute. Add the fish sauce, chicken, potatoes, and carrots. Stir-fry until chicken is reddish brown. Add the coconut milk and bring to a boil. Reduce heat, cover, and simmer for 30 minutes.

Yield: 4 servings

CRACKER BREAD SANDWICHES

3 rounds Middle Eastern cracker bread
(14-inch diameter)
10 ounces cream cheese, softened
1 package (6 ounces) alfalfa sprouts
4 ripe tomatoes, thinly sliced
4 avocados, peeled, pitted, and thinly sliced
2 medium-sized cucumbers, thinly sliced
12 ounces cheddar cheese, grated (3 cups)
1 can (12–14 ounces) black olives, chopped

Serve this as an appetizer or for lunch.

Follow package directions for preparing cracker bread.

Spread one layer of cracker bread with cream cheese; then layer the sprouts and tomatoes. Place another cracker on top and layer with avocados, cucumbers, cheddar cheese, and olives. Top with third cracker and cut into squares or wedges.

Yield: 10 to 12 servings

AIOLI CENTENNIAL CHICKEN

1 slice French bread, crust discarded
5 to 6 garlic cloves, crushed
2 egg yolks
1 teaspoon fresh lemon juice
pinch salt
pinch white pepper
¾ cup olive oil
4 whole, boneless, skinless chicken breasts
    (about 2½ pounds)
¼ teaspoon black pepper

This garlic lover's delight was created to help celebrate Idaho's Centennial in July of 1990. The aioli works best when made in a food processor; prepare it ahead and keep cold until ready to use.

To make aioli, soak bread in water and squeeze it dry. Place in food processor. Add garlic, egg yolks, lemon juice, salt, and white pepper. Purée mixture until smooth. With processor motor on, add olive oil slowly in a thin stream. Purée until mixture has the consistency of mayonnaise.

Cut chicken breasts in half. Lightly pound each until ½ inch thick. Spread aioli on both sides and sprinkle with pepper.

For Dutch oven cooking, place chicken in Dutch oven with maximum heat on top and broil until pieces are slightly browned and cooked thoroughly. For conventional cooking, place chicken in 2-quart casserole dish, bake uncovered at 400°F for 20 minutes, cover and reduce heat to 350°F, and bake for 10 more minutes.

Yield: 6 servings

GRILLED YOGURT-ENCRUSTED CORNISH HENS WITH COUSCOUS

2 cups plain, nonfat yogurt
2 tablespoons minced garlic
2 tablespoons chopped ginger root
2 tablespoons olive oil
¼ cup curry powder, or to taste
4 Cornish hens, split in half, with skin
    removed
1 package (10½ ounces) couscous, cooked
    according to package directions
plain yogurt, chopped fresh cilantro,
    chutney, chopped peanuts, and/or
    toasted sesame seeds for garnish

The yogurt marinade tenderizes the hens and forms a great crust during grilling. Chicken pieces may be used in lieu of Cornish hens.

In a food processor or with a whisk, combine yogurt, garlic, ginger root, and olive oil until smooth. Blend in curry powder. Pour over hens and marinate, covered, in refrigerator or cooler for 12 hours. Occasionally stir or shake container to coat thoroughly.

Remove from refrigerator or cooler about 30 minutes before cooking. In a Dutch oven grill over hot coals until browned and done, about 10 minutes on each side. Serve hot or at room temperature with prepared couscous and condiments such as plain yogurt, chopped cilantro, chutney, chopped peanuts, or toasted sesame seeds.

Yield: 4 to 8 servings

POLLY BEMIS CHICKEN

1 (3-pound) fryer chicken, cut in eight
    pieces
2 tablespoons olive oil
1 teaspoon salt
1 jar (8 ounces) orange marmalade
1 bottle (8 ounces) Russian dressing
1 fresh orange, peeled and thinly sliced

As a young Chinese woman, Polly Bemis was sold as a slave and later was won in a poker game by Charles Bemis, who eventually married her. Charles and Polly moved to the banks of the Salmon River in 1894, and Polly continued to live there until 1923. She was a hard worker, growing a productive garden, cutting firewood, cooking, and caring for livestock. Polly Creek on the Main Salmon River is named for her.

Brown chicken in oil in bottom of Dutch oven. Sprinkle with salt. Pour the marmalade and Russian dressing over chicken and arrange the orange slices on top.

Bake in Dutch oven for 40 to 45 minutes, or in 375°F conventional oven for 50 to 60 minutes.

Yield: 4 to 6 servings

SARA'S CHICKEN

8 chicken breasts, boned and skinned
1 cup plus ½ cup unbleached all-purpose
    flour
1 teaspoon freshly ground black pepper
½ cup olive oil
½ cup (1 stick) unsalted butter
oil for greasing pan
½ pound pancetta, diced
8 shallots, sliced
1½ pounds fresh mushrooms, sliced
1 cup tarragon vinegar
1 cup chicken broth
½ teaspoon dried tarragon
16 ounces mozzarella cheese, sliced
2 tomatoes, diced
¼ cup chopped fresh parsley

This unique Dutch oven dish is named after Sara Biddle, a special guest of Middle Fork River Tours. It's great served with fresh spinach fettuccine, Caesar salad, and steamed carrots.

Dredge chicken breasts in 1 cup of the flour and pepper; then brown them in a skillet in oil and butter. Place breasts in a lightly oiled Dutch oven.

In a separate pan, heat olive oil and sauté pancetta, shallots, and mushrooms until soft. Add ½ cup flour to mixture so it is sticky, not dry. Pour vinegar over mixture (most will evaporate). Pour chicken broth on top. At this point the mixture should be moist but not watery. Add tarragon.

Spoon mushroom mixture over chicken and place a slice of mozzarella over each breast.

Bake in Dutch oven for 35 minutes, or cover and bake in 350°F conventional oven for 30 to 40 minutes.

Top with tomatoes and parsley. Cover and cook for another 10 minutes.

Yield: 8 servings

BAKED WHEAT-GERM CHICKEN

1 large, three-drumstick frying chicken
½ cup (1 stick) unsalted butter, melted
1 cup wheat germ
salt and black pepper to taste
paprika to taste

Skin and dry the chicken pieces. Roll each in the melted butter and then dip into the wheat germ to coat. Place pieces in the bottom of a Dutch oven or in a baking dish. Pour remaining butter over chicken and season with salt and pepper. Garnish with paprika.

Bake for 40 to 45 minutes in the Dutch oven, or for 45 to 50 minutes in 350°F conventional oven.

Yield: 4 to 6 servings

CRAB-STUFFED CHICKEN BREASTS

4 large whole chicken breasts, halved,
    skinned, and boned
3 tablespoons plus 1 tablespoon unsalted
    butter or margarine
¼ cup unbleached all-purpose flour
¾ cup milk
¾ cup chicken broth
⅓ cup white vinegar
¼ cup chopped scallions
1 can (7½ ounces) crab meat
4 ounces fresh mushrooms, chopped
½ cup wheat germ
2 tablespoons fresh parsley, snipped
½ teaspoon salt
dash black pepper
4 ounces Swiss cheese, grated (1 cup)
½ teaspoon paprika

Place each chicken piece, boned side up, between two pieces of waxed paper. Working from the center out, pound each piece lightly with a meat mallet to make cutlet about ⅛ inch thick. Set aside.

In a saucepan, melt 3 tablespoons of the butter or margarine. Blend in flour.

In a separate bowl, stir together milk, chicken broth, and vinegar. Pour into butter-flour mixture in saucepan. Cook and stir until sauce thickens and bubbles. Set aside.

Sauté scallions in the remaining 1 tablespoon of butter until tender but not brown. Stir in crab meat, mushrooms, wheat germ, parsley, salt, and pepper. Stir in 2 tablespoons of the sauce. Top each chicken piece with about ¼ cup of the crab meat mixture. Fold sides in and roll up. Place rolls seam-side down in a Dutch oven. Pour remaining sauce over all.

Bake, covered, in 350°F conventional oven for 1 hour or until chicken is tender, or in Dutch oven with coals on top and underneath for 40 to 45 minutes. Uncover and sprinkle with cheese and paprika. Bake 2 minutes longer or until cheese melts.

Yield: 8 servings

COQ AU VIN

6 uncooked bacon slices, diced
⅔ cup sliced scallions
1 (about 2½ pounds) fryer chicken, cut up
    (or 3 breasts, halved, or 3 drumsticks
    and 3 thighs)
8 small white onions, peeled
8 ounces whole mushrooms
1 garlic clove, crushed
1 teaspoon salt
¼ teaspoon black pepper
½ teaspoon dried thyme
8 small potatoes, scrubbed
2 cups Burgundy wine
1 cup chicken broth
chopped parsley for garnish

In a Dutch oven or large skillet, sauté diced bacon and scallions until bacon is crisp. Remove and drain on a paper towel, leaving 2 tablespoons of bacon grease in skillet.

Put chicken pieces in skillet and brown well on all sides. Remove the chicken and set aside.

Put peeled whole onions, mushrooms, and garlic in Dutch oven or 2-quart casserole dish. Add the browned chicken pieces, bacon and scallions, salt, pepper, thyme, potatoes, wine, and chicken broth.

Bake for 1 hour in Dutch oven on medium heat, or cover and bake for 1 hour in 350°F conventional oven. Garnish with chopped parsley.

Yield: 6 servings

CRANBERRY STUFFING

4 cups cooked wild rice
2 cups raw cranberries, coarsely chopped
½ cup (1 stick) unsalted butter or margarine,
    melted
1 tablespoon grated yellow onion
3½ tablespoons sugar (optional)
½ teaspoon pepper
1 teaspoon salt (optional)
½ teaspoon mace
½ teaspoon dill weed
½ teaspoon dried thyme
½ teaspoon dried marjoram
1 garlic clove, minced

My sister-in-law Betty Mills uses this recipe as a stuffing or side dish for fowl.

Combine all ingredients and pour in Dutch oven or 1½-quart casserole dish.

Cook in Dutch oven over low heat for about 10 to 15 minutes, or in 350°F conventional oven for 15 minutes, until heated through. Allow to cool if using as a stuffing.

Yield: 6 to 8 servings

MUSHROOM-STUFFED CHICKEN BREASTS WITH ARTICHOKES

8 ounces fresh mushrooms, sliced
2 tablespoons plus 4 tablespoons margarine
6 to 8 chicken breasts, boned and skinned
½ teaspoon paprika
¼ teaspoon black pepper
1 package frozen artichoke hearts, thawed
    and drained
2 tablespoons unbleached all-purpose flour
⅔ cup chicken broth
⅔ cup dry sherry
salt to taste

Sauté mushrooms in 2 tablespoons of the margarine until browned. Place each chicken breast, boned side down, between two pieces of waxed paper. Pound each breast lightly with a meat mallet. Put mushrooms in the center of each breast, using all mushrooms, and roll up.

Heat 4 tablespoons margarine in a large skillet or Dutch oven, place breasts fold-side down in pan, and brown. Sprinkle breasts with paprika and pepper. Arrange breasts and artichokes in a Dutch oven or a large, shallow baking dish.

Stir flour into margarine remaining in pan and gradually add broth and sherry. Bring to boil, stirring constantly. Add salt to taste. Pour sauce over chicken and artichokes.

Bake 45 minutes in Dutch oven, or for 1 hour in 375°F conventional oven, basting occasionally.

Yield: 6 servings

STICKY CHICKEN

1 jar (8 ounces) apricot or pineapple jam
½ envelope dry Lipton onion soup mix
1 bottle (8 ounces) spicy French dressing
1 large chicken, cut into 8 pieces
salt and black pepper to taste

My aunt, Mac Oliver, found this recipe in her local newspaper. She often substitutes pheasant for the chicken, with delicious results.

Mix together the jam, dry soup, and French dressing. Chill for 1 hour or longer to blend the flavors.

Place chicken parts in a Dutch oven or 2-quart casserole dish and pour sauce over them. Season with salt and pepper to taste.

Bake in Dutch oven for 45 to 50 minutes, or cover and bake in 350°F conventional oven for 50 to 60 minutes, until tender.

Yield: 6 servings

CHICKEN MARBELLA

4 medium-sized whole chickens, quartered
1 head of garlic, peeled and minced
¼ cup dried oregano
salt and freshly ground black pepper to taste
½ cup vinegar
½ cup olive oil
1 cup pitted prunes
½ cup green olives
½ cup capers
4 bay leaves
1 cup brown sugar
1 cup chicke broth
¼ cup chopped fresh parsley

Thank you to Allison Lawrence for this "Yum-yum!" recipe that is always best the next day.

Combine chicken, garlic, oregano, salt, pepper, vinegar, olive, prunes, olives, capers, and bay leaves and marinate overnight.

Remove bay leaves from marinade. Arrange chicken in 12″ Dutch oven or baking pan, spoon marinade over the top, and sprinkle with brown sugar, broth, and parsley. Bake in a Dutch oven for 50 to 60 minutes, basting often. For conventional oven, bake at 350°F.

Yield: 10 to 12 servings

CHICKEN WITH DRIED FRUIT SAUCE

Chicken
4 (4 ounces each) skinned, boned chicken
    breast halves
½ teaspoon salt
¼ teaspoon black pepper
2 teaspoons margarine

Dried Fruit Sauce
1 cup mixed dried fruit bits
¾ cup white grape juice
¼ cup water
5 whole cloves
2 cinnamon sticks
1 tablespoon brown sugar
½ teaspoon cornstarch

Place chicken breasts between sheets of waxed paper and pound to ¼-inch thickness. Sprinkle breasts with salt and pepper.

Melt margarine in Dutch oven. Add chicken and cook 3 minutes on each side. Set chicken aside and keep warm.

Make the sauce: Add dried fruit bits, grape juice, water, cloves, and cinnamon sticks to Dutch oven and bring to boil. Add brown sugar and cornstach. Cook 1 minute, stirring constantly. Discard cloves and cinnamon sticks. Pour sauce over chicken before serving.

Yield: 4 servings

CREAMY CHICKEN ENCHILADAS

½ pound skinless, boneless chicken breasts, steamed or baked
1 package (10 ounces) frozen chopped spinach, thawed and well drained
¼ cup thinly sliced scallions
1 cup sour cream
¼ cup plain yogurt
2 tablespoons unbleached all-purpose flour
¼ teaspoon ground cumin
salt to taste
¼ cup milk
1 can (4 ounces) diced green chilies, drained
6 flour tortillas, 7-inch diameter
3 ounces Monterey Jack cheese, grated (⅓ cup)
salsa and chopped scallions for garnish

Shred cooked chicken into bite-size pieces. Combine chicken, spinach, and scallions; set aside.

In a separate bowl combine sour cream, yogurt, flour, cumin, and salt. Stir in milk and chilies. Divide sauce in half.

Combine chicken mixture and half the sauce. Divide this filling among the tortillas and roll them up. Place rolled tortillas in the bottom of a Dutch oven or baking pan. Spoon the remaining sauce over the enchiladas.

Bake in Dutch oven for 25 to 30 minutes, or in 350°F conventional oven for 30 minutes. Sprinkle with the cheese and let stand for 5 minutes. To serve, garnish with salsa and additional chopped scallions.

Yield: 6 servings

DAISY TAPPAN RICE DISH

2 cups uncooked brown rice
½ cup (1 stick) unsalted butter
1 cup chopped, pitted black olives
2 cans (10½ ounces each) chicken broth
4 ounces cheddar cheese, grated (1 cup)
2 fresh tomatoes, chopped (or 1 can, 28 ounces)
½ onion, chopped
½ green pepper, seeded and chopped
1 cup water

This recipe is named for Daisy Tappan, who came to the Middle Fork of the Salmon River to live when she was a child of seven. She was every bit as competent in the back country as any man who ever lived there, and spent most of her seventy years there, ranching and raising her family.

Combine all ingredients and mix well.

Bake in Dutch oven for 1 hour, or in 325°F conventional oven for 1½ hours.

Yield: 10 to 12 servings

CHICKEN AND ASPARAGUS STIR-FRY

1 pound boneless, skinless chicken breasts, cut into 1-inch thick strips
1 tablespoon plus 2 teaspoons cornstarch
1 teaspoon plus 2 teaspoons vegetable oil
¼ teaspoon salt
⅛ teaspoon freshly ground black pepper
½ pound fresh asparagus
1 cup chicken broth
1 teaspoon sugar
1 teaspoon sesame oil
1 teaspoon soy sauce
½ red bell pepper, finely chopped
1 piece (1 inch long) fresh ginger root, peeled and finely chopped
2 garlic cloves, finely chopped
¼ teaspoon cayenne pepper

Combine chicken, 1 tablespoon of the cornstarch, 1 teaspoon of the vegetable oil, salt, and black pepper. Cover and chill for 15 minutes.

In a large skillet or Dutch oven, heat ¼ inch of water to boiling. Break off woody ends of asparagus and cut each spear crosswise into 1-inch pieces. Add asparagus pieces to water and cook 2 to 3 minutes or until almost tender. Drain and set aside.

In a small bowl, combine broth, the remaining cornstarch, sugar, sesame oil, and soy sauce; set aside.

Heat the remaining 2 teaspoons vegetable oil and add red bell pepper and ginger root. Stir-fry 1 minute. Add garlic and cayenne and stir-fry another 30 seconds. Add chicken and stir-fry 3 minutes.

Stir in broth mixture and heat until thickened and chicken is cooked through, about 2 minutes. Stir in asparagus and heat through. Serve immediately.

Yield: 4 servings

MOM'S FAMOUS CASSEROLE

12 ounces wide egg noodles, cooked
2 cups diced, cooked chicken or turkey
1 can (10½ ounces) cream of chicken mushroom soup
2 large bunches of broccoli, cut into chunks
4 ounces cheddar cheese, grated (1 cup)
mayonnaise, if needed to moisten

Mary Jo Mulick's daughters, Emily and Mattie, named their favorite dinner for her. Mary Jo is a longtime friend of ours from Pocatello, Idaho.

Combine all ingredients in a Dutch oven or 1½-quart casserole dish.

Bake in Dutch oven for 30 to 40 minutes, or in 350°F conventional oven for 40 to 45 minutes.

Yield: 6 servings

MELISSA'S CHICKEN

4 whole chicken breasts, halved, skinned
    and boned
2 eggs, beaten
bread crumbs for coating chicken
unsalted butter and olive oil, for frying
16 ounces marinara sauce
½ cup milk
8 thin slices Swiss cheese
8 thin slices mozzarella cheese
2 ounces Parmesan cheese, grated (½ cup)

My longtime friend and river runner Melissa Green shared this easy, delicious Dutch oven chicken dish with me.

Dip chicken breasts in eggs and roll in bread crumbs to coat. Fry chicken in butter and olive oil.

In a small bowl, dilute marinara sauce with milk. Cover bottom of Dutch oven or 2-quart casserole dish with sauce mixture. Layer chicken on top of sauce. Top with slices of Swiss and mozzarella cheese. Sprinkle Parmesan over all.

Bake in Dutch oven for 30 minutes, or cover and bake in 350°F conventional oven for 30 minutes. Uncover partially and cook 10 more minutes.

Yield: 6 to 8 servings

CHICKEN WITH SHIITAKE MUSHROOMS

1 teaspoon vegetable oil
10 ounces shiitake mushrooms
2 medium shallots, minced
¼ garlic clove, minced
2 tablespoons white vinegar or chicken broth
2 tablespoons chopped fresh parsley
juice of ½ lemon
4 boneless chicken breasts, skin removed
2 tablespoons balsamic vinegar
10 ounces chicken stock or broth
2 tablespoons olive oil
1 tablespoon chopped fresh thyme
1 tablespoon chopped fresh tarragon
1 tablespoon chopped chives

Heat oil in a Dutch oven or ovenproof skillet until very hot. Sauté mushrooms, shallots, and garlic until wilted. Deglaze Dutch oven with vinegar or broth. Remove from heat and fold in parsley and lemon juice.

Cut a small pocket into the side of each chicken breast. Divide mushroom mixture into quarters and stuff into pockets. Tie with string to keep in place. Sauté breasts until golden on both sides.

Bake in Dutch oven for 10 to 12 minutes, or in 375°F conventional oven for 15 minutes. Remove chicken from Dutch oven or skillet; pour off excess fat.

Deglaze Dutch oven or skillet with vinegar and chicken stock or broth. Reduce drippings by half; then whip in olive oil, thyme, tarragon, and chives. Pour over chicken and serve.

Yield: 4 servings

LEMON CHICKEN NOODLE SOUP

1 tablespoon olive oil
3 carrots, peeled and chopped
2 stalks celery, chopped
1 medium onion, chopped
1 thick slice ginger root
1 teaspoon red pepper flakes
1 bay leaf
1 cup chicken broth
2 boneless chicken breasts, cooked and
    diced
1 tablespoon dried parsley flakes
1 tablespoon dried dill
2 quarts chicken broth
⅓ pound fine noodles
salt and freshly ground black pepper to taste
juice of 2 lemons

Thank you, Amie Bruggeman, my cousin from Boise, for this delicious soup recipe!

Heat Dutch oven or large pot over medium heat and add oil. Add carrots, celery, and onion and cook until softened, about 30 minutes. Add ginger root, red pepper flakes, bay leaf, and 1 cup of the chicken broth. Boil 2 minutes.

Add chicken, parsley, dill, and remaining broth. Heat to boil. Add noodles and simmer about 5 minutes. Remove bay leaf. Season with salt and pepper. Remove from heat; add lemon juice and serve.

Yield: 6 servings

ANGIE'S TURKEY CASSEROLE

2 packages (10 ounces each) frozen
    broccoli, thawed and drained
2 cups chopped, cooked turkey
1 can (10½ ounces) cream of chicken soup
½ cup mayonnaise
1 tablespoon lemon juice
½ teaspoon curry powder
2 ounces cheddar cheese, grated (½ cup)
½ cup bread crumbs
2 tablespoons unsalted butter, melted

My sister-in-law Angie Mills Cochran contributed this recipe.

Line a 12″ Dutch oven or a 9″ × 13″ baking pan with broccoli. Top with turkey.

In a separate bowl, mix chicken soup, mayonnaise, lemon juice, and curry powder. Pour over turkey. Mix cheese, bread crumbs, and butter, and sprinkle on top.

Bake in Dutch oven for 25 to 30 minutes, or in 300°F conventional oven for 30 minutes.

Yield: 6 to 8 servings

TURKEY AND BROWN RICE CASSEROLE

3 cups cooked turkey or chicken, cut in large
    chunks
3½ cups cooked brown rice
1 cup chopped onion
1 cup sliced celery
1 cup chopped green bell pepper
2 tablespoons plus 1 tablespoon margarine
1 can (10½ ounces) cream of mushroom
    soup
½ cup dry white wine or chicken broth
1 can sliced mushrooms, undrained
1 teaspoon dried sage leaves, crumbled
¼ teaspoon dried thyme leaves
½ teaspoon salt
dash black pepper
1 can (4 ounces) pimentos, drained and
    chopped
1 cup herb-seasoned croutons

Combine turkey and rice in Dutch oven or a 2½-quart casserole. Set aside.

Sauté onion, celery, and green pepper in 2 tablespoons of the margarine for 8 minutes, stirring frequently, until crisp-tender. Stir in soup, wine or broth, mushrooms, sage, thyme, salt, pepper, and pimentos. Pour mushroom-vegetable mixture over turkey and rice in Dutch oven or casserole. Stir with large spoon to combine.

Heat remaining 1 tablespoon margarine until melted. Toss croutons in melted margarine. Spoon around edge of Dutch oven. Bake with coals on top and underneath Dutch oven for 35 to 40 minutes, or in 350°F conventional oven for 40 to 45 minutes, until bubbly.

Yield: 8 servings

SWORDFISH WITH MUSTARD SAUCE

½ teaspoon finely chopped shallots
3 tablespoons vegetable broth
1 cup whipping cream
1½ tablespoons Dijon mustard
salt and black pepper to taste
4 (6 ounces each) swordfish fillets

Combine shallots and broth in a saucepan. Bring to a boil; then simmer until the liquid is reduced by one-third. Blend in whipping cream and mustard. Season with salt and pepper to taste.

Grill the swordfish until it is browned on both sides and the flesh flakes easily with a fork. Spoon mustard sauce over the fish to serve.

Yield: 4 servings

FISHMONGER TROUT

1 large cucumber, peeled and thinly sliced
1½ teaspoons plus 1½ teaspoons chopped
    fresh dill
1½ teaspoons plus 1 teaspoon fresh lemon
    juice
salt and black pepper to taste
1 cup sour cream
1 teaspoon lemon zest
2 trout fillets, 12 to 14 ounces each
2 tablespoons butter, melted

Line a 12″ Dutch oven with parchment paper.

Combine cucumber, 1½ teaspoons of the dill, and 1½ teaspoons of the lemon juice. Season with salt and pepper, and set aside.

In a separate bowl, combine sour cream, lemon zest, and remaining lemon juice and stir. Set aside.

Arrange fillets skin side down in Dutch oven or baking dish. Brush with butter. Bake in Dutch oven, or in 350°F conventional oven, until just opaque in center, about 10 minutes.

Divide cucumber mixture among four plates. Place half a trout fillet on top of each serving of cucumbers. Spoon sour cream sauce on top and sprinkle with remaining dill.

Yield: 4 servings

CHICKEN ENCHILADAS

2 pounds boned, cut-up chicken, cubed
2 tablespoons olive oil
1 bunch scallions, diced
1 small can (4 ounces) diced green chilies,
    drained
1 can (10 ounces) pitted black olives,
    drained and chopped
2 tablespoons cumin
salt to taste
2 cups sour cream
8 flour tortillas, 7-inch diameter
16 ounces Monterey Jack cheese, grated
    (4 cups)
8 ounces cheddar cheese, grated (2 cups)
1 can (8 ounces) tomato sauce

Brown chicken in oil in Dutch oven or skillet. Add scallions, and continue cooking until scallions are tender. Add chilies, olives, cumin, and salt; mix well. Fold in sour cream.

Cover the bottom of a Dutch oven or 9″ × 12″ casserole dish with tortillas. Put in one third of chicken mixture, one third of the cheeses, and one third of tomato sauce. Repeat this twice to make three layers. Cover the last layer with tortillas and sprinkle with cheese.

Bake in Dutch oven 40 to 45 minutes, or in 350°F conventional oven for 45 to 50 minutes. Let stand 10 minutes before serving.

Yield: 6 to 8 servings

BAKED RAINBOW TROUT

unsalted butter for greasing pan plus 2
    tablespoons
8 to 12 rainbow trout, cleaned, with or
    without heads and tails (use fillets of
    about 8 ounces each)
1 cup sliced mushrooms
4 scallions, sliced
2 garlic cloves, minced
2 cups whole wheat cracker crumbs
4 slices bacon, cooked and crumbled
½ teaspoon coarsely ground pepper
½ cup sliced almonds
1 small head of cabbage or lettuce

*Jerry Myers shared this unique recipe with me. Jerry would like
you to consider using commercially raised, cold-water trout in
order to limit the killing of wild trout. The cabbage leaves will
prevent the fish from sticking to each other or to the pan and add
a hearty flavor.*

Grease a 12″ Dutch oven or 9″ × 12″ baking dish and set aside.

Rinse trout and pat dry. Melt butter in a skillet and lightly
sauté mushrooms, scallions, and garlic. Mix in cracker crumbs,
bacon bits, pepper, and half of the almonds.

With a spoon, stuff about 2 heaping tablespoons of the
mushroom mixture into each trout. Tear off several leaves of
cabbage or lettuce and line the bottom of the Dutch oven or
dish. Place four stuffed fish on the leaves. Place another layer of
leaves, then another layer of fish. Repeat if you are cooking twelve
trout. Do *not* cover the top layer with leaves. Sprinkle with the
remaining almonds.

Bake in Dutch oven with 6 or 7 charcoals underneath and
15 to 20 on top of the oven, 25 to 35 minutes, leaving cover just
slightly ajar. If cooking conventionally, cover partially and bake in
375°F conventional oven for 35 to 40 minutes. Do not overcook.

Yield: 8 to 12 servings

STEAMED FISH WITH BLACK BEAN SAUCE

4 sea bass or other firm fish (about 2
    pounds total)
1 piece (1 inch long) fresh ginger root,
    peeled
4 tablespoons Chinese sesame oil
¼ cup plus 2 teaspoons soy sauce
2 scallions, cut into 1-inch pieces and
    slivered
½ cup canned black beans
1 tablespoon sherry (optional)

Wash the fish and pat dry with paper towel. Place in a large bowl.

Slice the ginger root into 12 thin slices, and then into slivers. Combine sesame oil, ¼ cup of the soy sauce, ¾ of the slivered ginger root, and scallions. Pour over fish.

Rinse black beans twice in warm water and drain well.

In a separate bowl, mince remainder of ginger root. Add beans and crush together. Add remaining 2 teaspoons soy sauce and the sherry, if desired. Rub mixture over fish.

Fill Dutch oven or 2-quart casserole dish 2 inches deep with water. Place fish in a shallow bowl or on a rack over simmering water.

Cook until the fish is done and flakes with a fork, 10 to 15 minutes in Dutch oven, or 20 to 25 minutes in 350°F conventional oven.

Yield: 4 servings

FLORENTINED SOLE

3 packages (10 ounces each) frozen
    spinach, thawed and drained
1 cup plus 1 cup sour cream
¼ cup chopped scallions
4 pounds sole fillets
salt and black pepper to taste
6 slices uncooked bacon
4 tablespoons dried parsley
paprika to taste (optional)

Combine spinach, 1 cup of the sour cream, and scallions in a bowl and mix well. Spread the mixture on the bottom of the Dutch oven and place the sole fillets on top. Add salt and pepper to taste. Spread remainder of sour cream on fillets and lay slices of bacon on top. Sprinkle with parsley and paprika, if desired.

Bake in Dutch oven for 30 to 40 minutes, or in 350°F conventional oven for 30 to 40 minutes.

Yield: 8 to 10 servings

HALIBUT WITH PINEAPPLE SALSA

Pineapple Salsa
½ cup diced pineapple
½ cup diced red bell pepper
¼ cup chopped cilantro
2 teaspoons minced jalapeño pepper
⅛ teaspoon salt
¼ cup fresh lime juice
1 teaspoon canola oil

Halibut
oil for greasing grill racks
1 teaspoon canola oil
4 (4 ounces each) halibut steaks (about 1
    inch thick)
⅛ teaspoon salt
lime wedges for garnish

Make the salsa: Combine pineapple, red pepper, cilantro, jalapeño, salt, lime juice, and oil. Stir well. Let stand 15 minutes, stirring occasionally.

Grease grill racks liberally.

Brush fish with 1 teaspoon oil and sprinkle with salt. Set aside.

Place fish on grill rack and cook 5 minutes on each side or until fish flakes easily with a fork. Serve with pineapple salsa and lime wedges.

Yield: 4 servings

SHRIMP QUICHE

pastry for 10-inch single-crust pie (recipe on
    page 161)
1 can (5½ ounces) whole shrimp, well
    drained
⅓ cup chopped scallions (tops included)
4 ounces Swiss cheese, grated (1 cup)
3 eggs
1 cup milk
½ teaspoon salt
⅛ teaspoon black pepper

Prepare the pastry recipe, or a pie crust mix.

Line the bottom of Dutch oven or 9″ pie dish with the pastry shell. Distribute shrimp over the bottom of pastry. Sprinkle evenly with the scallions and cheese.

In a separate bowl, beat together the eggs, milk, salt, and pepper. Pour over shrimp and cheese.

Bake in Dutch oven for 35 to 40 minutes, or in 350°F oven for about 45 minutes, until custard is firm in the center. Let stand for 10 minutes before serving.

Yield: 6 to 8 servings

YAMPA RIVER TRAPPER'S PIE

1 cup chopped onion

3 large russet potatoes, chopped and boiled

16 ounces frozen carrots and peas

3 tablespoons unsalted butter, melted

2 to 3 pounds pheasant or grouse, boiled, boned, and chopped

¼ teaspoon garlic powder

1 teaspoon dried sage

1 teaspoon dried oregano

salt and freshly ground black pepper to taste

4 teaspoons unbleached all-purpose flour

1½ to 2 cups milk

1½ to 2 cups chicken broth

1 can (10½ ounces) cream mushroom soup

pastry for 9-inch double-crusted pie (see recipe on page 161)

Gregg was a guide for us in the 1970s and 1980s and now owns Green River Drifters (greenriverdrifters.com), a fly-fishing outfitting business based in Steamboat Springs, Colorado. This is only one of Gregg's many great Dutch oven recipes.

In a large bowl, combine onion, potatoes, carrots and peas, and butter. Add the meat. Season with garlic powder, sage, oregano, salt, and pepper.

For the sauce combine flour, milk, and broth in a saucepan and stir well. Bring to a simmer over medium-high heat and cook until thickened. Add soup and combine.

Place pie dough in a 12″ Dutch oven or divide among three pie tins. Add filling and spoon sauce on top of pies, slightly mixing with filling.

Cover with top crust and flute edges. Make some slices in the top of the crusts. You can foil the edges so they don't burn.

Bake 1 hour. For a conventional oven, bake at 350°F for 1 hour.

Yield: 12 to 15 servings

SEAFOOD THERMIDOR

oil for greasing pan
1 pound fresh or frozen cod fillets
1 small onion, quartered
1 lemon slice
1 can (10½ ounces) cream of shrimp soup
3 tablespoons unbleached all-purpose flour
¼ cup milk
¼ cup vegetable broth
1 ounce mozzarella cheese, grated (¼ cup)
2 tablespoons snipped fresh parsley
½ cup soft bread crumbs
2 tablespoons grated Parmesan cheese
2 tablespoons margarine
½ teaspoon paprika

If you think that lobster Thermidor is the ultimate in good eating but you shudder at the cost, here's a delicious entree made in the same style but with cod, the "poor man's lobster."

Lightly grease a skillet or Dutch oven and set aside.

Thaw cod if frozen, and skin if necessary. Cut into ½-inch cubes. Place cod, onion, and lemon slice in skillet or Dutch oven. Add water to cover. Bring to boil, reduce heat, and simmer, covered, for 5 to 6 minutes or until fish flakes easily. Carefully drain fish well.

In a small saucepan, blend shrimp soup and flour. Gradually stir in milk and vegetable broth. Cook and stir until thickened and bubbly. Stir in mozzarella and parsley. Heat through. Fold fish into sauce. Spoon into four scallop shells or onto plates. If cooking in Dutch oven, place filled shells in bottom.

Combine bread crumbs, Parmesan, margarine, and paprika. Sprinkle over sauce.

Heat in covered Dutch oven to bubbling with heat on the top only, or broil in conventional oven 1 to 2 minutes, until cheese melts.

Yield: 4 servings

THALWEG STRUDEL

16 phyllo dough leaves
1 cup (2 sticks) unsalted butter, melted
1 pound scallops
6 ounces crab meat
1 pound fresh mushrooms, sliced
5 scallions, chopped
16 ounces cream cheese, softened
1 egg white
32 stalks fresh asparagus
2 cups Jiffy Hollandaise sauce (see
    recipe on page 84) or use dry instant
    hollandaise sauce

This once was the most asked-for recipe on the Rocky Mountain River Tours menu. We named it for a "thalweg," the deepest, fastest-moving channel in a river.

For each of eight strudels, lay out one of the phyllo leaves and brush with melted butter. Top with another leaf and brush that with butter also.

Mix scallops, crab meat, mushrooms, scallions, and cream cheese in a large bowl and place about 1 cup of the mixture at the end of the buttered phyllo leaves. Roll up, fold the sides over, and continue to roll. Place on baking sheet or in Dutch oven with open edge down. Do this with each strudel and brush them with egg white.

Bake in Dutch oven for 30 minutes, or in 375°F conventional oven for 30 to 40 minutes, or until golden brown.

Cut woody ends off asparagus and steam stalks.

Prepare hollandaise sauce. Garnish each strudel with asparagus and top with hollandaise.

Yield: 8 servings

SPAGHETTI SQUASH WITH SHRIMP SAUCE

1 spaghetti squash (about 2 pounds), cut in half lengthwise and seeded
1 tablespoon unsalted butter
1 large garlic clove, minced
1 medium-sized red bell pepper, seeded and cut in ¼-inch strips
1 medium-sized zucchini, cut in ¼-inch strips
1 cup chicken broth
1 teaspoon dried basil
hot pepper sauce to taste
salt to taste
freshly ground black pepper to taste
12 ounces cooked peeled shrimp, chopped
chopped fresh parsley for garnish
grated Parmesan cheese for garnish

Steam squash over boiling water for about 30 minutes. Using a fork, separate squash strands. Remove from heat and keep warm.

Melt butter in skillet and add garlic, bell pepper, and zucchini. Toss to coat. Sauté about 5 minutes or until vegetables are softened. Add chicken broth and basil. Season with hot pepper sauce, salt, and pepper, and bring to a boil. Add shrimp and cook until heated through.

Pour sauce over squash and toss to combine. Sprinkle with fresh parsley and serve with Parmesan cheese.

Yield: 4 servings

CARIBBEAN BEANS AND GRILLED THAI SHRIMP

1 jar (12 ounces) Thai peanut sauce (available at Asian markets)
24 large, fresh shrimp, peeled and cleaned
2 medium yellow onions, chopped
4 garlic cloves, crushed
1 tablespoon olive oil
2 cans red beans, drained
2 cans black beans, drained
1 small jar (8 ounces) tomatillo salsa
1 cup chopped cilantro
8 flour tortillas, 7-inch diameter

Pour peanut sauce over shrimp and marinate in refrigerator for 2 hours or overnight.

Sauté onions and garlic in oil until soft. Add beans. Cook until heated through. Mash partially. Add salsa and cilantro. Spread over tortillas and roll up.

Put shrimp on skewers and grill for 5 minutes on outdoor grill. Serve with tortillas and Papaya Salsa (recipe on page 79).

Yield: 8 servings

STUFFED SCAMPI

12 large shrimp, peeled and cleaned
1 onion, chopped
2 cups chopped celery
½ cup unsalted butter
12 ounces tiny shrimp
¼ teaspoon minced garlic
¼ teaspoon dried thyme
1 tablespoon chopped fresh parsley
1 tablespoon tomato sauce
3 tablespoons vegetable broth
4 ounces Parmesan cheese, grated (1 cup)
1 cup dried bread crumbs
2 tablespoons unsalted butter, melted

Butterfly the shrimp by cutting in half lengthwise, but *don't cut all the way through.*

Sauté onion and celery in butter until onion is golden. Add the tiny shrimp and sauté 5 to 7 minutes, until just cooked. Remove from heat. Add garlic, thyme, parsley, tomato sauce, vegtable broth, and Parmesan cheese. Mix until blended. Add bread crumbs and sauté another 3 minutes. Cool.

Arrange the shrimp, cut side up, in a Dutch oven or 2-quart casserole dish. Pile stuffing on each shrimp to cover completely. Brush with melted butter.

Bake in Dutch oven for 10 to 15 minutes, or in 350°F conventional oven for 10 to 15 minutes, or until shrimp are cooked through.

Yield: 4 to 6 servings

FETA SHRIMP BAKE

1¼ cups chopped onion
4 garlic cloves, minced
⅛ cup olive oil
6 fresh tomatoes, chopped
½ cup chopped fresh parsley
1 tablespoon chopped fresh basil
2 teaspoons fresh marjoram
2 teaspoons grated lemon peel
salt and freshly ground black pepper to taste
1 teaspoon allspice
3 pounds shrimp, peeled and cleaned
1½ pounds feta cheese, crumbled
1 pound linguine pasta, cooked

This is always a favorite dish on Rocky Mountain River Tours' Middle Fork float trips.

In a Dutch oven or skillet, sauté onion and garlic in oil. Add tomatoes, parsley, basil, marjoram, and lemon peel. Simmer about 10 minutes. Season with salt, pepper, and allspice. If preparing conventionally, pour mixture into 2-quart casserole dish.

Put the shrimp on top of mixture. Sprinkle with feta cheese.

Bake in Dutch oven for about 20 minutes, or in 350°F conventional oven for 30 to 40 minutes, until the shrimp is done. Serve on top of linguine.

Yield: 8 servings

SALMON RIVER LASAGNA

1 can (7½ ounces) salmon, drained
1 cup ricotta cheese
6 ounces Parmesan cheese, grated (1½ cups, divided)
4 ounces cream cheese
1 egg
1 pound fresh sfoglia pasta sheets, uncooked (or 6 cooked and drained lasagna noodles)
6 ounces mozzarella cheese, grated (1½ cups)
1 cup spaghetti sauce (your favorite)
½ package (5 ounces) frozen spinach, thawed and drained

This is an easy salmon recipe from my sister, Marcia Colliat. It adapts very well to a Dutch oven.

Remove any skin and bones from the salmon and flake.

Mix ricotta cheese, ½ cup of the Parmesan, cream cheese, and egg.

If using sfoglia, slice the sheets of pasta lengthwise into thirds. Line the bottom of a 12″ Dutch oven or 9″ × 12″ baking dish with a layer of pasta. Top with half of the cheese mixture, half of the salmon, ½ cup of the mozzarella cheese, half of the spaghetti sauce, and half of the spinach. Place another layer of pasta over the top, and repeat other layers.

Bake in Dutch oven for 20 to 30 minutes, or in 350°F conventional oven for 35 to 45 minutes.

Sprinkle with remaining ½ cup mozzarella and 1 cup Parmesan. Bake 5 more minutes. Let stand for a few minutes before slicing.

Yield: 8 servings

EASY FISH BAKE

olive oil or unsalted butter for greasing pan
½ cup Miracle Whip
½ cup cream cheese
3 tablespoons fresh lemon juice
2 tablespoons minced garlic
⅓ cup grated Parmesan cheese
1 teaspoon seafood seasoning
4 white fish filets (6 to 8 ounces each)
½ cup Italian bread crumbs
kosher salt to taste

Fred and Shane Hughes gave my old friend Gail Siemen from Pocatello this recipe. They live to fish.

Combine Miracle Whip, cream cheese, lemon juice, garlic, Parmesan cheese, and seafood seasoning and spread on one side of each filet. Sprinkle filets with bread crumbs and kosher salt.

Place in single layer in lightly greased 12″ Dutch oven and bake for 20 to 25 minutes or until fish flakes with a fork. For a conventional oven, place fish in an oiled pan and bake at 350°F.

Yield: 4 servings

SALMON SOUFFLÉ

unsalted butter for greasing pan plus 3
    tablespoons
3 tablespoons unbleached all-purpose flour
1 teaspoon salt
dash freshly ground black pepper
1 cup milk
1 can (16 ounces) salmon, drained and
    flaked
2 tablespoons lemon juice
1 tablespoon grated onion
3 tablespoons chopped fresh parsley
3 eggs, separated

Butter a Dutch oven or 1½-quart casserole dish.

Melt butter in a skillet and blend in flour, salt, and pepper. Gradually add milk and cook on low heat, stirring all the while, until thickened. Add salmon, lemon juice, onion, and parsley.

In a separate bowl, beat egg yolks until thick and lemon-colored. Gradually stir eggs into salmon mixture. Mix well.

Beat egg whites until stiff and fold gently into salmon mixture. Turn into Dutch oven or casserole dish.

Bake in Dutch oven for about 35 to 40 minutes, or in 375°F conventional oven for about 50 minutes.

Yield: 6 servings

SPAGHETTI WITH CLAMS

1 pound spaghetti
2 tablespoons olive oil
6 cloves garlic, minced
1 small dried chili pepper, crumbled, or
    pinch of red pepper flakes
4 pounds clams, scrubbed
1 cup bottled clam juice
2 tablespoons coarsely chopped fresh
    flat-leaf parsley, plus whole leaves for
    garnish
juice of 1 lemon
3 tablespoons unsalted butter
coarse salt and freshly ground black pepper
    to taste

Cook spaghetti according to package directions until slightly underdone. Drain, reserving 1 cup of cooking liquid. Set aside.

Heat Dutch oven or large skillet over medium heat and add oil. Add garlic and chili pepper; cook until garlic is golden, about 2 minutes. Add clams and clam juice, and raise heat to high. Bring to a boil, cover, and cook, shaking occasionally, 2 to 3 minutes, until clams open. Stir in parsley. Transfer to a bowl and set aside.

Return Dutch oven or skillet to medium-high heat. Add reserved pasta water and lemon juice. Reduce until slightly thickened, about 2 minutes. Remove from heat and whisk in butter. Add clam mixture and spaghetti. Cook over medium-low heat until heated through, 2 to 3 minutes. Season with salt and pepper; garnish with parsley.

Yield: 6 servings

SALMON CHEESE CASSEROLE

1 can (16 ounces) salmon, with liquid
1 can (4 ounces) mushrooms, drained and
    sliced, or 4 ounces fresh
1½ cups bread crumbs
2 eggs, beaten
4 ounces cheddar cheese, grated (1 cup)
1 tablespoon lemon juice
1 tablespoon minced onion

Flake fish in a bowl, removing all bones. Add all remaining ingredients and mix thoroughly. Pour into Dutch oven or 1½-quart casserole dish.

Bake in Dutch oven for 30 to 35 minutes, or in 350°F conventional oven for 35 to 40 minutes.

Yield: 6 servings

SALMON WITH CUCUMBER SALAD AND DILL SAUCE

6 tablespoons sour cream
2 tablespoons plus 1 teaspoon finely
    chopped fresh dill
3 tablespoons rice vinegar
1½ tablespoons minced shallots
¼ teaspoon lemon zest
2 teaspoons fresh lemon juice
1 garlic clove, minced
4 wild salmon filets (4 to 6 ounces each,
    about 1-inch thick)
¼ teaspoon salt
¼ teaspoon freshly ground black pepper
1 tablespoon olive oil
¼ cup vegetable broth
2 cups thinly sliced cucumber (about
    1 pound)

Combine sour cream, 2 tablespoons dill, 2 tablespoons vinegar, shallots, lemon zest, lemon juice, and garlic in a bowl, stirring well; cover and chill.

Season filets evenly with salt and pepper. Heat 12″ Dutch oven or a large skillet over medium-high heat and add olive oil. Add fish to pan and cook for 3 minutes. Turn fish and cook 1 more minute. Remove from heat. Add broth; cover and let stand 3 minutes or until fish flakes easily when tested with a fork.

Combine cucumber, 1 tablespoon vinegar, and remaining dill in a bowl; toss gently to coat. Place about ½ cup cucumber mixture on each of four plates; top each serving with 1 filet and 2 tablespoons sour cream mixture.

Yield: 4 servings

BAKED WRAPPED TILAPIA

1-inch cube fresh ginger root, finely
    chopped or grated
2 garlic cloves, finely chopped or grated
2 green onions (green part only), finely
    chopped
1 jalapeño pepper, seeded and chopped
1 cup finely chopped cilantro
2 tablespoons safflower oil
dash of toasted sesame oil
dash of soy sauce
dash of fish sauce
4 teaspoons dark maple syrup
salt and freshly ground black pepper to
    taste
4 fresh tilapia filets (4 ounces each), or
    other firm-fleshed whitefish

A delicious, healthy dinner from Allison Lawrence.

Combine ginger root, garlic, green onions, jalapeño, cilantro, oils, soy sauce, fish sauce, and maple syrup in a bowl. Season with salt and pepper to taste.

Place each filet on a piece of foil or parchment paper and divide topping evenly among them, spreading it over the top. Fold foil to form a packet and seal the edge.

Put packet in a 12" Dutch oven and bake 25 to 30 minutes. For a conventional oven, bake at 400°F for 20 minutes.

Yield: 4 servings

Meat Dishes

Remember

When a recipe calls for baking, braising, stewing, or roasting, the Dutch oven must be covered with charcoal briquettes on top of the lid. For boiling, frying, sautéing, and quick heating, leave the Dutch oven cover off. For more on cooking techniques for the Dutch oven, see "Dutch Oven Care and Use," pages 2–4. When using a conventional oven, preheat the oven to the given temperature.

Guacamole

4 ripe, large avocados
1 cup chopped scallions
2 cups chopped cilantro
2 tomatoes, chopped
1 jar (10 ounces) picante sauce
3 tablespoons garlic powder
1 teaspoon black pepper
juice of 1 lemon
1 head of lettuce, shredded, for garnish

Assembly

2 pounds pork, beef, or chicken, cut into
    ½-inch chunks (may use hamburger)
1 red onion, chopped
1 can (4 ounce) diced jalapeños (use less
    for medium heat)
24 corn tortillas, 8-inch diameter
2 bell peppers, seeded and chopped
2 tomatoes, chopped
16 ounces cheddar cheese, grated (4 cups)

ESPECIAL DEL RIO DE HOMBRE POBRE

"The poor man's river special" was devised by Gregg Tipton for a fishing trip down the Green River in Utah a few years ago. Its ease of preparation was an instant hit with all Gregg's cohorts, since their main task of the evening was chasing Mr. Wily Trout!

Make the guacamole: Peel and pit avocados. Mash in large bowl. Add scallions, cilantro, and two chopped tomatoes. Add picante sauce to taste, garlic powder, pepper, and lemon juice. Mix well. Cover and keep cool until ready to serve.

Sauté the meat. After 3 to 5 minutes, add one-third of the chopped red onion and the jalapeños. Cook until meat is rare.

In a circular pattern, layer bottom of a 12″ Dutch oven or 2-quart casserole dish with eight to twelve of the tortillas, with edges of tortillas coming 2 to 3 inches up the sides of dish. Add meat mixture, spreading evenly. Add another layer of four to six tortillas placed up to the edges of the dish. Add peppers, two chopped tomatoes, and the rest of the onion. Spread evenly. Cover with eight or so more tortillas.

Bake in Dutch oven for 20 minutes, or cover and bake in 350°F conventional oven for 20 minutes. Sprinkle with cheese and bake another 5 to 10 minutes.

Cut in wedges and serve topped with lettuce and guacamole.

Yield: 6 to 8 servings

BETTY'S BEEF AND POTATO BAKE

4 cups peeled, thinly sliced potatoes
1 cup plus ¼ cup chopped yellow onion
1 teaspoon salt
⅛ teaspoon plus 1 teaspoon black pepper
1 teaspoon dried parsley flakes
1 pound ground beef
¾ cup milk
½ cup rolled oats
¼ cup tomato sauce

Thanks to my sister-in-law, Betty Mills, from Coeur d'Alene, Idaho, for contributing this recipe.

Arrange potatoes, 1 cup of the chopped onion, salt, ⅛ teaspoon pepper, and parsley flakes evenly in Dutch oven or loaf pan.

In a separate bowl, mix ground beef, milk, oats, tomato sauce, ¼ cup onion, and 1 teaspoon pepper. Pour over potato mixture in Dutch oven or pan.

Bake in Dutch oven for 25 to 30 minutes, or in 350°F conventional oven for 30 to 40 minutes.

Yield: 4 servings

PEGGY'S LAMB

1 garlic clove
2 teaspoons fresh marjoram
½ teaspoon salt
2 tablespoons lemon juice
½ teaspoon Tabasco
leg of lamb, 3 to 4 pounds
20 small pimento-stuffed green olives
2 strips uncooked bacon, cut in ½-inch
    pieces

This is the main dish that won the 1988 World Championship Dutch Oven Cookoff, a major event of the Festival of the American West in Logan, Utah. It was prepared by Rosemary Parkinson and Peggy Roskelley of Smithfield, Utah.

Mash and mix together garlic, marjoram, and salt. Add lemon juice and Tabasco.

Make ten holes in lamb leg with sharp narrow knife, as far as you can cut without cutting through the meat. Push a green olive into each hole, then a piece of bacon, ½ teaspoon of the garlic mixture, and then another stuffed olive. Repeat until all holes are filled.

For Dutch oven cooking, roast in 12″ Dutch oven with about ten coals underneath and eighteen around the rim of the top, for 3 hours. For conventional cooking, bake in covered 2-quart casserole dish in 350°F conventional oven for 3 hours. Garnish with parsley, or serve with stir-fried vegetables heaped around the meat.

Yield: 8 servings

BAKED ZITI

2 tablespoons olive oil
4 ounces thinly sliced pancetta, chopped
2 pounds Boston butt pork shoulder, cut into
 1¼-inch cubes
salt and freshly ground black pepper to taste
1 pound Italian hot sausages, casings
 removed and sliced
2 cups chopped onion
¾ cup chopped carrot
2 stalks celery, chopped
6 fresh thyme sprigs
6 garlic cloves, chopped
2 bay leaves
½ teaspoon (or to taste) dried crushed red
 pepper
2 cups beef broth
1 can (28 ounces) chopped plum tomatoes,
 juice reserved
1 can (12 ounces) crushed tomatoes
1¼ pounds ziti pasta
8 ounces whole-milk mozzarella cheese,
 coarsely grated (2 cups)
2 ounces Parmesan cheese, grated (½ cup)

Hearty and plenty to go around, this is an awesome spring river trip meal from river guide and nurse, Keri O'Connor from Pocatello, Idaho. Make this sauce ahead of time and freeze. It will hold up great in your cooler and make this meal easy to prepare on the river.

Heat Dutch oven or heavy large pot over medium-high heat and add oil. Add pancetta and sauté until brown and crisp. Using slotted spoon, transfer pancetta to bowl. Season pork with salt and pepper. Add half of pork to drippings in pot; sauté until brown. Transfer pork to bowl with pancetta. Repeat with remaining pork.

Add sausage and sauté until no longer pink, breaking up with back of fork. Add onion, carrot, celery, thyme, garlic, bay leaves, and crushed red pepper. Sauté until vegetables are tender, about 10 minutes. Add broth and bring to boil, scraping up browned bits. Return pancetta and pork with any accumulated juices. Add chopped tomatoes with juice along with crushed tomatoes. Cover and simmer until pork is very tender, about 2 hours. Adjust heat as needed to maintain gentle simmer and stir occasionally.

Uncover pot; tilt to one side and spoon off fat from surface of sauce. Remove bay leaf. Season sauce to taste with salt and pepper.

Cook pasta in a large pot according to package directions until tender but firm to bite, stirring occasionally. Drain pasta; mix into sauce.

Sprinkle with both cheeses. Bake until heated through and golden, about 20 minutes. For a conventional oven, place mixture in a 9″ × 13″ baking dish and bake at 350°F for 30 minutes.

Yield: 6 servings

BUNCE'S CHICKEN AND CHOPS

6 tablespoons olive oil
12 pork chops, trimmed of fat
12 chicken thighs, skinned
12 chicken breasts, skinned
lots of coarsely ground black pepper
1 teaspoon garlic powder
1 can (15 ounces) Contadina sweet-and-
    sour sauce
1 large onion, chopped
2 green peppers, seeded and chopped
4 ounces fresh mushrooms, chopped

Mike Bunce created this sweet-and-sour dish, which was a favorite among his river buddies. He liked to cook it long and slowly so that everything fell apart.

Heat oil in Dutch oven or large skillet. Brown pork chops and chicken with pepper and garlic powder (may have to do in batches). Layer in large Dutch oven or 2-quart casserole dish and pour sweet-and-sour sauce over the top. Add onion, green peppers, and mushrooms.

Bake in Dutch oven with mostly top heat for 40 to 50 minutes, or cover and bake in 350°F conventional oven for 45 to 50 minutes, until meat falls off the bones.

Yield: 15 servings

SALMON RIVER STEW

2 pounds beef chuck, cut in 1½-inch cubes
1 pound ground pork sausage
2 cups hot water
1 garlic clove
3 medium onions, sliced
2 bay leaves
1 tablespoon salt
2 teaspoons black pepper
6 carrots, sliced
4 potatoes, cubed
2 green peppers, seeded and chopped
6 fresh tomatoes, cubed
8 ounces cheddar cheese, grated (2 cups)

Brown beef and sausage in a skillet or Dutch oven. Drain well. Add hot water, garlic, onions, bay leaves, salt, pepper, carrots, potatoes, green peppers, and tomatoes.

Cover and simmer for 45 to 50 minutes, stirring occasionally to keep from sticking. Remove bay leaves and garlic clove.

Cook another 10 minutes or until vegetables are tender. Sprinkle cheese on top and cover; heat until cheese melts.

Yield: 8 to 10 servings

SHIITAKE LASAGNA

unsalted butter for greasing pan
1 ounce dried shiitake mushrooms
2 cups warm water
2 pounds fresh mushrooms, finely chopped
¼ cup olive oil
¼ cup plus ½ cup unsalted butter
1 medium-sized onion, finely chopped
1 can (14 ounces) Italian plum tomatoes,
    drained and chopped (can use fresh)
½ cup chopped fresh parsley
⅓ cup unbleached all-purpose flour
2 cups milk
1 teaspoon nutmeg
dash of salt
1 pound fresh sfoglia pasta sheets,
    uncooked (or 6 cooked and drained
    lasagna noodles)
6 ounces prosciutto, thinly sliced
8 ounces Parmesan cheese, grated (2 cups)
paprika and ground black pepper to taste

Butter a 12" Dutch oven.

Stem the shiitake mushrooms and soak for at least 30 minutes in warm water. Reserving the water, remove mushrooms and chop them. Strain shiitake liquid through a sieve lined with paper towels.

Cook fresh mushrooms in olive oil and ¼ cup of the butter until liquid is reduced to almost nothing. Add the shiitake mushrooms, onion, tomatoes, and parsley. Cook for 15 minutes, partially covered.

To make the sauce, melt remaining ½ cup butter and add flour gradually. Stir 5 minutes over low heat. Slowly stir in milk and liquid from shiitake mushrooms. Cook until thickened and smooth, about 10 to 12 minutes. Add nutmeg and salt.

If using sfoglia, cut each sheet of pasta lengthwise into three strips. Place in bottom of Dutch oven or 9" × 12" baking pan, slightly overlapping strips. Layer with mushroom mixture, sauce, and prosciutto. Sprinkle with Parmesan. Top should be covered with one last layer of pasta and topped with rest of sauce and cheese. Sprinkle with paprika and pepper.

Bake in Dutch oven for 20 to 25 minutes, or bake uncovered in 350°F conventional oven for 35 to 45 minutes. Lasagna should be golden brown on top. Let stand 10 minutes before serving.

Yield: 10 to 12 servings

MOROCCAN COUSCOUS OF LAMB, FRUIT, AND VEGETABLES

⅔ cup uncooked couscous
⅔ cup dried currants
½ cup chicken stock
¼ cup olive oil
10 ounces lean boneless lamb, cut into
    1-inch cubes
4 large garlic cloves, minced
salt to taste
1 apple, peeled, cored, and cut into 6
    pieces
1 red bell pepper, seeded and cut into
    1-inch pieces
6 medium scallions, cut into thirds
6 carrots, peeled and cut into 1-inch lengths
¼ cup pine nuts
2 teaspoons fresh lemon juice
1 teaspoon cinnamon
¼ teaspoon cayenne pepper

Place couscous and currants in small bowl. Bring chicken stock to a boil and pour over couscous and currants. Stir with fork, cover bowl, and set aside.

Heat olive oil in Dutch oven. Sauté and stir lamb, garlic, and salt in oil. Reduce heat and add apple, bell pepper, scallions, and carrots. Cover and cook until lamb is no longer pink.

Add pine nuts, lemon juice, cinnamon, and cayenne, tossing gently to blend. Cover and cook until just heated through. Adjust seasoning and serve over couscous.

Yield: 6 servings

CHEF'S HATS

6 frozen puff pastry shells
6 ounces cheddar cheese, grated (1½ cups)
3 tablespoons unbleached all-purpose flour
3 eggs, lightly beaten
1 package (10 ounces) frozen chopped
    spinach, thawed and drained
4 ounces fresh mushrooms, sliced
6 crisply cooked bacon slices, crumbled
½ teaspoon salt
dash black pepper

Roll out each pastry shell into a 6- to 8-inch circle. Line paper muffin cups with each circle of dough, so that edges of dough stand up at least a ½-inch above the cup edge.

Toss cheese with flour. Add eggs, spinach, mushrooms, bacon, salt, and pepper. Mix well. Fill the cups with cheese mixture.

Bake in Dutch oven for 25 to 30 minutes, or in 350°F conventional oven for 40 minutes.

Yield: 6 servings

CLAIR'S DUTCH OVEN ENCHILADAS

2 pounds ground beef
1 onion, diced
1 green bell pepper, seeded and diced
seasoned salt to taste
1½ tablespoons plus 4 tablespoons ground
    cumin
ground black pepper to taste
1 can (28 ounces) tomato sauce
1 can (12 ounces) tomato paste
1 can (10 ounces) enchilada sauce
    (medium-hot)
1 dozen corn tortillas, 8-inch diameter
10 fresh mushrooms, sliced
1 medium ripe avocado, peeled, pitted, and
    diced
3 fresh tomatoes, cut into 8 sections each
2 pounds sharp cheddar cheese, grated
    (8 cups)
1 head lettuce, torn in leaves
sour cream and hot sauce for garnish

Variations: You can replace the ground beef with chopped and browned round steak. To make this dish vegetarian, replace beef with brown rice held together with mozzarella cheese and seasoned with cumin. Or make an enchilada pie with the same ingredients, in four layers, using three tortillas cut into fourths to start each layer. Bake the same way in a Dutch oven or casserole.

Clair Yost, who gave me this special recipe, has been boating for fun and profit for a number of years. He has a special knack for cooking in a Dutch oven.

Brown the beef with onion and green pepper. Pour off grease. Season to taste with seasoned salt, 1½ tablespoons cumin, and pepper.

In a separate pan, heat tomato sauce, tomato paste, enchilada sauce, and remaining 4 tablespoons cumin. Simmer for 5 minutes.

Dip each of six tortillas into the heated sauce to make it soft. Lay each tortilla on a plate and spread beef mixture across the middle of each. Put several mushrooms, a spoonful of avocado, two tomato sections, and several spoonfuls of grated cheese on top of beef for each tortilla. Roll up tortillas to make enchiladas. Place six rolled enchiladas in a 12″ Dutch oven or 9″ × 12″ baking dish, fold-side down.

Pour some sauce over top of enchiladas; spread remaining cheese over sauce. Repeat process with remaining six tortillas, and stack on top of others. Put any remaining meat mixture, vegetables, and cheese on top. Cover.

For Dutch oven cooking, line the outside of the lid with charcoal briquettes, place four briquettes in the center, and place eight briquettes underneath. Bake 30 minutes, checking center and making sure the heat is not too hot. Bake 15 to 20 minutes more. Take coals off and let stand 10 minutes before serving.

For conventional cooking, bake uncovered in 350°F oven for 45 to 50 minutes.

Serve enchiladas on beds of lettuce leaves. Top with sour cream and hot sauce.

Yield: 6 to 8 servings

NICKY'S LASAGNA

1 pound ground beef
1 onion, minced
6 cups cottage cheese
10 lasagna noodles, cooked al dente
1 large can (28 ounces) tomato sauce
1 small can (6 ounces) tomato paste
2 teaspoons dried sweet basil
2 teaspoons dried oregano
½ cup beef broth
16 ounces mozzarella cheese, sliced or
    grated (4 cups)
8 ounces fresh mushrooms, sliced
grated Parmesan cheese for garnish

Variation: To make this dish vegetarian, substitute 1 pound raw zucchini for the beef. Sauté the onions in a little olive oil.

Bill Caccia gave me this recipe, which we made part of the menu on our Main Salmon River float trips.

Brown the ground beef and onion in skillet or Dutch oven. Drain off fat.

Place half of beef-onion mixture in bottom of Dutch oven or 9″ × 12″ baking dish. Spread half the cottage cheese over beef. Cover with half the lasagna noodles. Cover noodles with half the tomato sauce and half the tomato paste. Sprinkle with half the sweet basil and oregano and ¼ cup of the broth. Repeat the layer.

Bake in Dutch oven for 30 to 35 minutes, or in 350°F conventional oven for 35 to 40 minutes. Sprinkle with mozzarella cheese and cover with mushrooms. Bake 10 more minutes (if baking in conventional oven, leave cover off for last 10 minutes). Serve with Parmesan cheese.

Yield: 6 to 8 servings

PORK CHOPS WITH SPINACH DUMPLINGS

6 rib, sirloin, or blade pork chops
salt and black pepper to taste
½ cup chopped onion
1 garlic clove, minced
1¾ cups plus ¼ cup tomato juice
1 can (8 ounces) mushroom stems and
    pieces, drained
1 teaspoon sugar
½ teaspoon salt
dash black pepper
¼ teaspoon dried thyme, crushed
¼ teaspoon dried marjoram, crushed
¼ teaspoon dried rosemary, crushed
1 egg, beaten
1 package (10 ounces) frozen chopped
    spinach, thawed and drained
⅓ cup fine dry bread crumbs or wheat germ
1 ounce Parmesan cheese, grated (¼ cup)
1 tablespoon unsalted butter, melted
2 tablespoons unbleached all-purpose flour

Trim excess fat from chops. Cook fat trimmings in Dutch oven or skillet until 2 tablespoons drippings accumulate. Discard fat pieces. Season chops with salt and pepper and brown in hot drippings. Remove chops and set aside.

In the same Dutch oven or skillet, cook onion and garlic until onion is tender but not brown. Add 1¾ cups of the tomato juice, mushrooms, sugar, salt, pepper, thyme, marjoram, and rosemary. Return chops to pan. Simmer, covered, for 20 to 25 minutes.

Meanwhile, combine egg, spinach, bread crumbs, Parmesan, and butter in a separate bowl. Place 2 tablespoons of spinach mixture atop each chop to form a dumpling. Simmer, covered, until dumplings are heated through, 10 to 15 minutes. Place chops and dumplings on a platter.

In a small bowl, blend flour with the remaining ¼ cup tomato juice. Stir into pan juices. Cook and stir until thickened and bubbly. Pour sauce over chops.

Yield: 6 servings

BOEUF BOURGUIGNON

6 strips uncooked bacon, cut in ½-inch
    pieces
3 pounds beef rump or chuck, cut in
    1½-inch cubes
1 large carrot, peeled and sliced
1 medium onion, sliced
1½ teaspoons salt
⅛ teaspoon black pepper
3 tablespoons unbleached all-purpose flour
1 can (10½ ounces) condensed beef broth
1½ cups beef broth
1 teaspoon tomato paste
4 garlic cloves, minced
1½ teaspoons dried thyme
1 bay leaf
8 ounces small white onions, peeled
1 pound fresh mushrooms, sliced
2 tablespoons margarine

Cook bacon in Dutch oven or skillet until crisp. Remove bacon. Add beef cubes and brown well in the bacon fat. Remove browned beef and set aside. Brown carrot and onion. Season with salt and pepper. Stir in flour. Add condensed broth and mix well.

Put beef back in Dutch oven, or place all in 2-quart casserole dish. Add cooked bacon, remaining broth, tomato paste, garlic, thyme, bay leaf, and onions.

Bake in Dutch oven for 45 minutes on medium heat, or cover and bake in 350°F conventional oven for 45 minutes.

Meanwhile, sauté mushrooms in margarine. Add mushrooms to Dutch oven or casserole; cook 15 more minutes. Remove bay leaf before serving.

Yield: 6 to 8 servings

SAUSAGE-STUFFED ACORN SQUASH

2 large acorn squash, cut in half
salt to season squash
1 pound bulk pork sausage
1 cup chopped celery
½ cup sliced fresh mushrooms
¼ cup chopped onion
1 egg, slightly beaten
½ cup sour cream
1 ounce Parmesan cheese, grated (¼ cup)
¼ teaspoon salt

Scoop the seeds out of the four halves of squash. Lightly salt inside of each squash. Place squash in Dutch oven or 9" × 12" baking pan. Bake in Dutch oven for about 25 to 30 minutes, or in 350°F conventional oven for 30 minutes, until tender.

Combine sausage, celery, mushrooms, and onion in skillet. Sauté until vegetables are tender and meat is brown. Drain well.

Combine egg, sour cream, Parmesan, and ¼ teaspoon salt in a separate bowl. Stir into sausage mixture. Fill each squash half with sausage mixture and place halves in Dutch oven or 2-quart casserole dish.

Bake in Dutch oven for 15 to 20 minutes, or cover and bake in 350°F conventional oven for 20 minutes.

Yield: 4 to 6 servings

SAVORY RICE AND RED BEANS

1 slice uncooked bacon, chopped
1 cup chopped onion
1 can (14½ ounces) chicken broth
¾ cup brown rice, uncooked
¾ cup celery, sliced
¼ teaspoon salt
¼ teaspoon hot pepper sauce
⅛ teaspoon ground black pepper
1 can (15½ ounces) dark red kidney beans,
    with liquid
1 small green bell pepper, seeded and cut
    into bite-size strips

Serve this dish on its own or stuff the mixture into warm tortillas with salsa.

Cook bacon until crisp. Drain bacon, reserving 1 teaspoon of the drippings. Cook onion in reserved bacon drippings until tender. Add bacon, broth, rice, celery, salt, hot pepper sauce, and pepper. Bring to boil; then reduce heat. Cover and simmer for 40 minutes.

Add kidney beans with their liquid, and pepper strips. Simmer, covered, for 5 minutes.

Yield: 6 servings

SHIRLEY'S MEDITERRANEAN CHOPS

2 tablespoons olive oil
1 large white onion, chopped
6 garlic cloves, minced
6 boneless pork chops, 6 ounces each
salt and freshly ground black pepper to taste
1 teaspoon dried oregano
1 cup unbleached all-purpose flour
1 can (20 ounces) diced tomatoes,
    undrained
1½ cups sliced pimento-stuffed green olives
cooked rice or pasta
Parmesan cheese

Shirley Henry, wife of Bob Henry, is a longtime river runner from Boise, Idaho.

Preheat 12″ Dutch oven over medium-high heat and add 1 tablespoon olive oil. Add onion and sauté until soft. Add garlic and sauté 1 minute.

Season the chops with salt and pepper. Mix together oregano and flour. Dredge pork chops in flour and place on platter. Set aside.

Remove onion and garlic from Dutch oven and set aside. Add the rest of the olive oil. Brown the pork chops on both sides. Return onion and garlic to Dutch oven and add tomatoes with juice and olives.

Bake for 30 minutes. For conventional oven, place pork chops and sauce in a 2-quart casserole dish and bake at 375°F for 30 minutes.

Serve over rice or pasta with Parmesan cheese grated over the top.

Yield: 6 servings

STUFFED PORK CHOPS

Stuffing

1 tablespoon margarine
6 fresh mushrooms, sliced
½ cup sliced scallions
¾ cup cooked brown rice
1 tablespoon soy sauce
¼ teaspoon ground ginger

Pork Chops

6 large pork chops, 1 inch thick
3 tablespoons unbleached all-purpose flour
¼ teaspoon garlic salt
¼ teaspoon dry mustard
black pepper to taste
1 egg, lightly beaten
⅓ cup fine bread crumbs
3 tablespoons margarine

Make the stuffing: Melt 1 tablespoon margarine. Add the mushrooms and cook until tender. Add the scallions and rice. Stir in soy sauce and ginger. Remove from heat.

Trim the fat from the pork chops and cut a pocket in the side of each. Stuff each pocket with about 3 tablespoons of the stuffing. Secure pockets with skewers or toothpicks.

Combine the flour, garlic salt, mustard, and pepper. Dredge each chop in the flour mixture to coat all sides. Dip in egg, then in bread crumbs.

Melt 3 tablespoons margarine in a skillet. Add the chops and cook over low heat until brown on all sides, about 40 to 45 minutes, turning them over halfway through cooking time.

Yield: 6 servings

WITCHES' BREW

1 pound uncooked bacon
1 pound hamburger
1 cup diced celery
1 cup diced onion
1 can (28 ounces) tomatoes
2 cans red kidney beans
1 can mushrooms
1 cup egg noodles, uncooked

Fry bacon and hamburger in Dutch oven or large skillet. Drain off fat. Add celery, onion, tomatoes, beans, mushrooms, and noodles.

Bake 45 minutes in Dutch oven, or 1 hour in 350°F conventional oven.

Yield: 8 to 10 servings

SWEET STEAK

2 pounds round steak, cut in serving-size
    pieces
1 cup unbleached all-purpose flour for
    dredging
2 tablespoons olive oil
salt to taste
black pepper to taste
½ cup minced onion
1 cup brown sugar
1 can (8 ounces) tomato sauce
1 can (10½ ounces) pizza sauce
2 cups water
2 tablespoons dried parsley flakes
flour or cornstarch for thickening (optional)

*My aunt, Mac Oliver, gave me this recipe. She usually serves it
with buttered noodles. This recipe was a winner about ten years
ago in a Montana CowBelles beef cook-off.*

Pound steak until tender. Dredge each piece in flour and brown
in oil in Dutch oven or skillet. Salt and pepper to taste. If
cooking conventionally, move steak to 2-quart casserole dish.

In a separate bowl, mix onion, brown sugar, tomato sauce,
pizza sauce, water, and parsley flakes. Pour sauce over steak.

Simmer slowly in Dutch oven for about 1½ hours, or cook
covered in 325°F conventional oven for 1½ hours. If necessary,
add flour or cornstarch to thicken gravy.

Yield: 6 servings

PORK'S COMPANION

1½ pounds ground beef
8 ounces ground pork
2 eggs, beaten
½ cup wheat germ
½ cup bread cubes
1 can (8 ounces) tomato sauce
¼ cup finely chopped onion
¼ cup chopped green pepper
¼ cup chopped celery
1 tablespoon Worcestershire sauce
dash dried thyme, crushed
½ teaspoon dried oregano
½ teaspoon dried sage
1 teaspoon salt

*This was a favorite recipe of my late good friend, Jim Mulick, who
rafted rivers with me for years. Jim's meat loaf is as spicy as his
personality was, and he felt the secret ingredient is the pork.*

Combine all ingredients and mix well. Shape mixture into a loaf
and place in Dutch oven or 9″ × 9″ baking dish.

Bake in Dutch oven for 1 hour at moderate heat, or in 350°F
conventional oven for about 1¼ hours.

Yield: 6 to 8 servings

TAMALE PIE

1 medium onion, chopped
1 garlic clove, minced
2 tablespoons vegetable oil
1 pound lean ground beef
8 ounces bulk pork sausage
1 can (28 ounces) tomatoes
1 can (16 ounces) whole-kernel corn,
  drained
1 tablespoon chili powder
½ teaspoon cumin
½ teaspoon oregano
1 cup pitted ripe olives, drained (these may
  be whole or sliced)
1 small can (7¾ ounces) tomato sauce
2 cans (15 ounces each) Nalley tamales,
  corn husks removed, cut into 1- or
  2-inch chunks
4 ounces cheddar cheese, grated (1 cup)

This is also good served cold on lettuce leaves, similar to a taco salad.

Sauté onion and garlic in vegetable oil in Dutch oven or skillet until golden but not brown. Add ground beef and bulk sausage and continue sautéing until meat is brown. Drain off excess fat.

Stir in tomatoes, corn, chili powder, cumin, and oregano. Cover and simmer 10 minutes. If cooking conventionally, move mixture to 2-quart casserole dish.

Add olives, tomato sauce, and tamales. Sprinkle the top with grated cheddar cheese.

Bake in Dutch oven for about 45 minutes, or bake uncovered in 350°F conventional oven for 45 minutes, until cheese is melted and meat mixture is bubbly.

Yield: 6 servings

SAUSAGE ROLL

1 loaf frozen bread dough
1 pound ground pork sausage
½ yellow onion, chopped
4 ounces sharp cheddar cheese, grated
    (1 cup)
2 egg yolks
2 egg whites
1 ounce Parmesan cheese, grated (¼ cup)

Sheri Farr makes this recipe ahead of time and keeps it in the freezer in case she has overnight guests. She uses it the most when she has all the guys at the house during hunting season.

Following the package instructions, let the dough rise until doubled in size.

Brown the sausage and onion in a large skillet. In a medium bowl, combine cheddar and egg yolks. Add egg yolk mixture to sausage mixture; mix together, set aside, and cool slightly.

Roll out bread dough to ½-inch thickness (about 10″ × 12″ rectangle). Spread the sausage mixture in the center of the bread dough leaving a 1-inch border around the edges; roll up. Cut slits in the roll. Brush with egg whites and sprinkle with Parmesan cheese.

Place in a 12″ Dutch oven and bake for 20 minutes. For a conventional oven, place roll on cookie sheet and bake at 350°F for 15 to 20 minutes until golden brown. At this point you can wrap it and freeze it for future use.

Yield: 6 servings

RICE WITH SAUSAGE, APPLES, AND PRUNES

1½ cups uncooked wild rice
1¼ cups uncooked white rice
3 tablespoons unsalted butter
1½ cups chopped onion
6 ounces smoked sausage, cut into ½-inch
    cubes
5 cups plus 1 cup canned chicken broth
9 ounces pitted prunes, chopped
¼ teaspoon dried thyme, crumbled
¾ teaspoon salt
2 medium-sized green apples, peeled,
    cored, and cut into ½-inch pieces
salt to taste
black pepper to taste

Cook wild rice in boiling water for 10 minutes. Drain and set aside. Repeat for white rice: Cook in boiling water for 10 minutes, drain, and set aside.

Melt butter in Dutch oven or large skillet, add onions, and sauté until soft. Add sausage, wild rice, and white rice, and stir. Mix in 5 cups of the chicken broth, prunes, thyme, and salt. Bring mixture to boil, stirring occasionally. Reduce heat, cover, and cook 30 minutes.

Add apples. Cover and cook until all broth is absorbed and rice is tender, adding remaining 1 cup broth if needed. Season with salt and pepper.

Yield: 6 to 8 servings

BASQUE (SPANISH) RICE

⅓ to ½ cup olive oil
1 onion (Walla Walla sweet, preferably),
    chopped
5 garlic cloves, chopped
12 ounces Basque chorizo, sliced
5 medium garden tomatoes, diced, or 2
    cans (15 ounces each) diced tomatoes
4 green bell peppers, seeded and chopped
2 to 3 jalapeño peppers, seeded and
    minced (optional)
8 cups water
4 cups white rice
salt and freshly ground black pepper to taste

Great river trip recipe from our Basque friend Louis Uranga of Boise, Idaho.

Heat Dutch oven or other large heavy pot over medium-high heat and add oil. Add onions and sauté until golden. Add garlic and sauté 1 minute. Add chorizo, tomatoes, bell peppers, and jalapeños (if using) and cook 5 minutes.

Add water and bring mixture to boil. Add rice, return to a boil, and reduce heat to a simmer. Season with salt and pepper to taste. Cover and stir occasionally.

When rice is 5 minutes from done, remove from heat and keep covered. Let it sit for 10 minutes and serve.

Yield: 8 to 10 servings

SPICY PESTO LASAGNA

2½ pounds bulk sausage
1 pound fresh pasta sfoglia sheets,
    uncooked (or 8 cooked and drained
    lasagna noodles)
2 jars (10 ounces each) pesto sauce
12 tomatoes, sliced
4 cups plain yogurt
2 pounds Monterey Jack cheese, grated
    (8 cups)
6 ounces Parmesan cheese, grated
    (1½ cups)

Variation: This recipe is just as delicious when made without the sausage.

Brown sausage in Dutch oven or skillet. Drain off fat.

Arrange one layer of pasta in each of two Dutch ovens or in a 9″ × 12″ baking dish. Spread each layer with one-fourth of the pesto (use half the pesto in 9″ × 12″ pan). Break up one-fourth of the sausage (half the sausage for 9″ × 12″ pan) thinly and evenly over pesto. Layer a third of the tomato slices over sausage. Spread with half of the yogurt and sprinkle with half of the Monterey Jack and Parmesan. Add another layer of pasta and repeat layers of pesto, sausage, tomato slices, yogurt, and cheeses. Cover top layer with sliced tomatoes and sprinkle with Parmesan.

Bake in Dutch oven 35 to 40 minutes, or bake uncovered in 350°F conventional oven for 45 to 50 minutes, until golden and bubbly. Spoon off excess olive oil. Let stand 10 minutes before serving. Cut into squares.

Yield: 10 to 15 servings

BOBNOXIOUS CHILE VERDE

1 tablespoon olive oil
1 large yellow onion, chopped
4 garlic cloves, minced
2 pounds boneless pork rib meat, cut into
    bite-size cubes
juice of 2 lemons
juice of 4 limes
1 can (6 ounces) hot Herdez chile verde
    sauce (or mild if you prefer)
1 cup water, as needed
1 teaspoon ground cumin
1 cup coarsely chopped fresh cilantro
Asadero cheese
tortillas or cooked rice

Bob Henry worked as a river guide for us and lives in Boise, Idaho, with his wife, Shirley. We are still not certain why the other guides referred to such a sweet guy as "Bobnoxious"!

Heat Dutch oven over medium-high heat and add oil. Sauté onion until soft. Add garlic and sauté 1 minute. Add pork and brown, being careful not to burn the onion and garlic. Add citrus juices and bring to a simmer. Add chile verde sauce and enough water to just cover the pork. Add the cumin and stir.

Bake about 30 minutes or until the pork falls apart and the liquid has been reduced. Add the cilantro and cook about 5 minutes more, stirring. For a conventional oven, bake at 350°F for 30 minutes.

Serve with Asadero cheese on tortillas (homemade are best) or with rice.

Yield: 6 servings

SENSATIONAL STEAK FAJITAS

¾ pound lean flank steak
2 teaspoons cumin
2 teaspoons chili powder
¼ teaspoon salt
⅛ teaspoon garlic powder
⅛ teaspoon black pepper
⅛ teaspoon cayenne pepper
4 flour tortillas, 8-inch diameter
1 teaspoon canola oil
2 cups diced onion
⅓ cup green bell pepper strips
⅓ cup red bell pepper strips
⅓ cup yellow bell pepper strips
1 tablespoon lime juice
sour cream
salsa and cilantro sprigs for garnish

Trim fat from steak. Slice diagonally across grain into thin strips. Combine steak, cumin, chili powder, salt, garlic powder, black pepper, and cayenne pepper in a zip-top bag. Seal bag and shake well to coat.

Wrap tortillas in foil and heat in Dutch oven or warm conventional oven, or wrap in paper towels and heat in microwave.

Heat oil in skillet. Add steak, onion, and bell peppers and stir-fry for 6 minutes or until steak is medium rare. Remove from heat and add lime juice. Divide mixture among tortillas and roll up. Serve with sour cream, salsa, and cilantro.

Yield: 4 servings

HORSERADISH-ENCRUSTED PORK LOIN ROAST

1 pork loin roast, 3 pounds, rolled, tied
salt and freshly ground black pepper
1 tablespoon olive oil
¾ cup toasted bread crumbs
3 tablespoons prepared horseradish
3 tablespoons Dijon mustard

Spicy Apricot Sauce
1 jar (18 ounces) apricot preserves
⅓ cup fresh lime juice
1 garlic clove, chopped
½ teaspoon ground cumin
1 pinch cayenne pepper (or to taste)
⅛ teaspoon salt

Season pork with salt and pepper. Heat olive oil in Dutch oven or frying pan and brown roast on all sides over medium-high heat. Remove from heat and let cool.

In medium bowl, combine bread crumbs with horseradish and set aside. Completely cover pork with Dijon mustard and then pat the crumb mixture on until pork is covered.

Place in Dutch oven and roast for 1 hour or until a thermometer inserted in center registers 160° or pork is still slightly pink. For a conventional oven, roast at 350°F for 50 to 60 minutes.

Slice and serve with warm Spicy Apricot Sauce.

Blend all ingredients in a food processor at home. When ready to use, bring to boil in heavy saucepan. Simmer 1 minute. Stir well. Serve immediately on the sliced pork.

Yield: 6 to 8 servings

Meatless Dishes

Remember

When a recipe calls for baking, braising, stewing, or roasting, the Dutch oven must be covered with charcoal briquettes on top of the lid. For boiling, frying, sautéing, and quick heating, leave the Dutch oven cover off. For more on cooking techniques for the Dutch oven, see "Dutch Oven Care and Use," pages 2–4. When using a conventional oven, preheat the oven at the given baking temperature.

TOMATO AND GARLIC PIZZA

oil for greasing pans
Sage and Olive Focaccia Bread (unbaked)
    (see recipe on page 53)
½ cup chopped fresh basil
8 garlic cloves, thinly sliced
1½ cups sliced fresh mushrooms
4 thinly sliced fresh tomatoes
freshly ground black pepper to taste
6 ounces Parmesan cheese, grated
    (1½ cups)

Grease two Dutch ovens or two pizza pans or baking sheets.

Divide the dough in half and press into the two Dutch ovens or two pizza pans or baking sheets, turning the edge of the dough over on itself to form a lip. Layer basil, garlic, mushrooms, and tomatoes on top of dough. Sprinkle with pepper and Parmesan.

For Dutch oven cooking, bake for 25 minutes with about fifteen coals underneath the oven and coals covering the lid. For conventional cooking, bake in 375°F conventional oven for 20 to 25 minutes.

Yield: 2 pizzas

SWEET-AND-SOUR CABBAGE

2 heads red cabbage
2 apples
1 onion, chopped
1 tablespoon caraway seeds
1 tablespoon salt
½ tablespoon black pepper
2 cups water
1 cup sugar
½ cup white vinegar
½ cup (1 stick) unsalted butter

Werner Rosenbaum donated this recipe, which was given to him by his mother. Most people do not care for cooked cabbage; however, Werner claims that he has never served this to anyone who has not enjoyed it and asked for seconds!

Chop cabbage and apples into coarse pieces. Add onion, caraway seeds, salt, and pepper. Cook in simmering water until cabbage is tender. Do not overcook. Drain off any remaining water. Add sugar and vinegar. Add butter and stir until melted. Serve hot.

This dish can be prepared ahead of time, frozen and reheated. If you choose this option, add the butter when reheating.

Yield: 10 servings

SWEDISH BAKED BEANS

1 apple
¼ cup raisins
¼ cup molasses
½ cup chopped onion
¾ cup ketchup
1 tablespoon prepared mustard
¼ cup sweet pickle relish
¾ cup sugar
1 can (16 ounces) baked beans (Brick Oven variety preferred)

This is a delicious recipe from my Aunt Mac in Billings, Montana.

Grind apple, raisins, molasses, and onion together; if you don't have access to a food processor, finely chop these ingredients. Mix well with ketchup, mustard, relish, and sugar. Blend into baked beans.

Bake 1 hour in Dutch oven at medium heat, or 1½ hours in 225°F conventional oven.

Meat variation: Grind an 8-ounce piece of cooked ham in with the other ingredients.

Yield: 6 to 8 servings

SPRING VEGETABLE RISOTTO

1 tablespoon olive oil
1 onion, diced
1 garlic clove, chopped
1½ cups arborio rice
5 cups (approximately) chicken stock
¼ cup each very finely chopped leek, carrot, zucchini
1 bunch fresh thyme, chopped
1 cup (2 sticks) butter
2 ounces Parmesan cheese, finely grated (½ cup)
salt and freshly ground black pepper to taste
1 tablespoon truffle oil

Larry and Jan Schlicht, friends from Boise, shared a recipe from their son, Chef Eric. If desired, top risotto with a single large seared scallop.

Combine oil and onion in Dutch oven or large pot. Cook over medium heat until onion is soft. Add garlic and cook 1 minute. Add rice and sauté about 3 to 5 minutes.

Deglaze pot with 1 cup of the stock and cook until it is almost evaporated; add half of remaining stock and cook until reduced by half. Add the rest of the stock and reduce by half.

Stir in vegetables, thyme, and butter, and cook 5 minutes. Stir in cheese and season with salt and pepper and finish with truffle oil.

Yield: 4 servings

TOFU CACCIATORE

several garlic cloves, sliced
1 large onion, sliced
1½ teaspoons fresh oregano leaves
1½ teaspoons fresh sweet basil, chopped
1 teaspoon fresh parsley
1 teaspoon anise seeds
1 cup mushrooms, cut in half
3 tablespoons plus 1 tablespoon olive oil
1 package (14 ounces) firm tofu
3 cans (6 ounces each) tomato paste
5 cans (8 ounces each) tomato sauce
1 cup water
1 can (6 ounces) pitted black olives, drained
2 tablespoons sugar
½ teaspoon salt
½ teaspoon black pepper
2 tablespoons grated Parmesan cheese
5 whole bay leaves

This is Bill Caccia's delicious vegetarian adaptation of his brother John's Chicken Cacciatore (page 90).

In a large Dutch oven, sauté garlic, onion, oregano, basil, parsley, anise seeds, and mushrooms in 3 tablespoons olive oil. Set aside.

Cut tofu into ½- to 1-inch cubes. In a skillet, sauté tofu in remaining 1 tablespoon oil until golden brown.

In a separate bowl, mix tomato paste, tomato sauce, water, olives, sugar, salt, pepper, Parmesan, and bay leaves. Add the tofu and the tomato sauce mixture to the Dutch oven. Simmer for 3 hours. Remove bay leaves before serving.

If you prepare the sauce ahead of time and freeze, do not prepare the tofu until the last minute.

Yield: 6 servings

BLACK BEAN BURRITOS

12 flour tortillas, 10-inch diameter
3 cups drained canned black beans
1½ cups finely chopped red onion
3 cups grated Monterey Jack cheese
3 avocados, peeled, pitted, and cut into chunks
6 tablespoons chopped cilantro
1 cup salsa

Working with one tortilla at a time, spread ¼ cup of black beans in the center. Top beans with 1 tablespoon of the onion and ¼ cup Monterey Jack. Roll tortilla gently to enclose filling. Repeat for all tortillas. Transfer the burritos, seam sides down, to a Dutch oven or 9″ × 12″ baking pan, forming one layer.

Bake in Dutch oven for 15 to 20 minutes, or in 350°F conventional oven for 15 to 20 minutes. Top each burrito with avocado, cilantro, and salsa.

Yield: 12 servings

PASTA FRITTATA

8 ounces uncooked spaghetti
2 tablespoons plus 1 tablespoon unsalted
    butter, softened
8 teaspoons olive oil
½ cup finely chopped onion
1 can (32 ounces) peeled Italian plum
    tomatoes, chopped and drained
6 ounces mozzarella cheese, grated (1½
    cups)
2 ounces Parmesan cheese, grated (½ cup)
salt and freshly ground black pepper to taste
½ cup pine nuts, toasted
½ cups chopped fresh basil
5 eggs
2 teaspoons plus 2 tablespoons minced
    fresh Italian parsley

If you want to serve an appetizer or light entree that will delight your guests, this is the one! You may even come up with your own variation.

Cook spaghetti. Drain and mix with 2 tablespoons of the butter in a large bowl. Cool.

Heat olive oil in skillet and add onion. Cook until tender and golden brown. Add tomatoes and cook until mixture is thick. Cool to room temperature.

Stir mozzarella cheese and half of the Parmesan into the tomato mixture. Season with salt and pepper. Stir pine nuts and basil into tomato-cheese mixture. Set aside.

Beat five eggs in a large bowl. Stir in the spaghetti, remaining Parmesan, and 2 teaspoons of the parsley.

Heat 1 tablespoon of the butter in a 12″ Dutch oven or skillet over high heat. Spread half of the pasta-egg mixture evenly in Dutch oven or pan and cook 1 minute, shaking pan to prevent sticking. Reduce heat.

Spread a third of the tomato-cheese mixture over the pasta-egg mixture, leaving a ½-inch outside border. Top with remaining pasta-egg mixture, spreading to edges of pan. Cook until mixture is almost set and bottom is golden brown, about 3 to 5 minutes.

Place under broiler about 2 inches from heat, or, in Dutch oven, heat from the top only, covering the lid with briquettes as if to broil. Cook until frittata is set and golden brown. If you are making this in a skillet, invert the frittata after broiling, put it back into the skillet, and brown the other side.

Sprinkle 2 tablespoons parsley over frittata. Cut into wedges to serve. You can make this dish 2 hours ahead and serve it at room temperature.

Yield: 8 to 10 servings

OLYMPIC SPUDS

4 large Idaho baking potatoes
2 cups sour cream
4 to 6 large garlic cloves, minced
1 teaspoon freshly ground black pepper
¼ teaspoon cayenne pepper, plus more for additional seasoning
1 teaspoon Parsley Patch seasoning, all-purpose blend (or use any salt-free blend of herbs) plus more for additional seasoning
1 bunch broccoli, chopped
1 red onion, chopped
1 pound fresh mushrooms, chopped
4 tablespoons unsalted butter

I created this potato dish during the 1996 Summer Olympics and received a gold medal from my guests!

Bake the potatoes for 45 to 60 minutes in Dutch oven, or for 1 hour in 350°F conventional oven. Cool potatoes until they can be handled.

Cut each potato in half lengthwise and scoop the insides into a bowl. Beat insides with sour cream, garlic, black pepper, cayenne, and 1 teaspoon Parsley Patch seasoning until fluffy and smooth. Spoon into potato shells and place in Dutch oven or 9″ × 12″ baking pan.

Bake in Dutch oven for 15 to 20 minutes, or in 350°F conventional oven for 15 to 20 minutes, until heated through.

Sauté broccoli, onion, mushrooms, cayenne pepper, and Parsley Patch in butter until tender. Spoon on top of the potatoes and serve.

Yield: 8 servings

HERB-BROILED TOMATOES

¾ cup shredded whole wheat cereal, crushed fine
1½ tablespoons minced fresh parsley
½ teaspoon dried basil
⅛ teaspoon garlic powder
1 tablespoon unsalted butter, melted
3 medium tomatoes
fresh parsley sprigs for garnish

Combine cereal, parsley, basil, and garlic powder in a small bowl. Add butter and stir well. Set aside.

Cut tomatoes in half crosswise. Place halves, cut-side up, in a Dutch oven or baking pan. Place under broiler, or, in Dutch oven, heat from the top only, covering the lid with briquettes as if to broil, for 10 minutes. Sprinkle with cereal mixture. Broil tomatoes again until lightly browned. Garnish with parsley sprigs.

Yield: 6 servings

ITALIAN ZUCCHINI BAKE

1 tablespoon olive oil
½ cup chopped onion
3 cups shredded zucchini (squeeze out all
    excess moisture)
1¼ cups rolled oats
1 ounce mozzarella cheese, grated (¼ cup)
1 egg, slightly beaten
½ teaspoon dried basil, crushed
½ teaspoon salt (optional)
¼ teaspoon freshly ground black pepper
⅓ cup tomato sauce

Heat olive oil in 10″ Dutch oven or skillet, add onion, and sauté until tender. Transfer onion to large bowl and add zucchini, oats, mozzarella cheese, egg, basil, salt, and pepper. Mix well. Pour mixture into Dutch oven or 1½-quart casserole dish. Spread tomato sauce evenly over the top.

Bake in Dutch oven for 30 minutes, or in 350°F conventional oven for 30 minutes.

Yield: 6 to 8 servings

GOOD OLD-FASHIONED DUTCH-OVEN POTATOES

4 slices uncooked bacon (optional), cut into
    bite-sized pieces
1 tablespoon vegetable oil (optional)
1 medium onion, sliced
5 pounds medium potatoes, sliced
½ cup chopped mushrooms
1 can (10½ ounces) cream of mushroom
    soup
½ cup sour cream
8 ounces cheddar cheese, cubed or grated
    (2 cups)

Neil and Carrie Dabb of Logan, Utah, shared this award-winning recipe with me. The Dabbs won first place at the World Championship Dutch Oven Cookoff in Logan in 1989.

Cook bacon in Dutch oven until nearly done (if not using bacon, preheat a small amount of oil before proceeding). Add onion and cook until light brown in color, stirring occasionally. Add potatoes and stir. Cover and let cook until potatoes are tender, about 30 minutes.

Add mushrooms, cover, and cook 3 to 5 minutes.

Add mushroom soup and sour cream. Cook 2 to 3 minutes longer.

Spread cheese on top, cover, and remove from heat. Let stand 5 to 10 minutes or until cheese melts.

Yield: 8 to 10 servings

POLENTA WITH WILD MUSHROOMS

6½ cups water
1½ tablespoons salt
2 cups coarse-grained polenta
2 tablespoons unsalted butter
2½ tablespoons olive oil
4 shallots, peeled and minced
1 pound golden chanterelle mushrooms,
    or other wild mushrooms, washed and
    dried
salt and freshly ground black pepper to taste
¼ cup chopped fresh chives
⅓ cup freshly grated Parmesan cheese

Put water and salt in a Dutch oven or saucepan; bring to a simmer. Add polenta in a thin stream, stirring constantly. Cook on low heat for about 20 minutes; polenta is ready when it pulls away from the side of the pan. Pour onto waxed paper to set up.

Heat butter and olive oil in a skillet and sauté shallots. Add chanterelles and cook until they have absorbed the butter and oil. Add salt and pepper. Cook another 15 minutes. Add chives just before mushrooms are ready.

Cut polenta in squares or wedges, and top with mushrooms and Parmesan.

The polenta can be prepared ahead of time, frozen, and reheated. To do so, freeze polenta with waxed paper between each piece. To reheat, put 1 tablespoon oil in skillet and add polenta. Turn polenta after 1 or 2 minutes and remove when heated through.

Yield: 6 servings

FOCACCIA AND CHÈVRE PIZZA

4 ounces mild chèvre, such as Montrachet,
    coarsely crumbled
2 tablespoons chopped fresh basil
1 baked plain focaccia, 10-inch diameter
    (recipe on page 44)
12 Kalamata olives, pitted and sliced
12 large radicchio leaves
4 teaspoons olive oil

Prepare focaccia as instructed on page 44.

Sprinkle chèvre and basil over focaccia. Top with olives and half of the radicchio leaves. Drizzle with olive oil. Place in Dutch oven or on pizza pan or baking sheet.

Heat in Dutch oven or in 350°F conventional oven for 5 to 10 minutes, until cheese melts and bread is warmed through. Top with remaining radicchio.

Yield: 6 small servings

SWEET CHEESE PATOOTIES

6 medium sweet potatoes
3 ounces extra-sharp cheddar cheese,
    shredded (¾ cup)
3 ounces mozzarella cheese, shredded
6 tablespoons raisins
6 tablespoons Grape-Nuts cereal

The extra-sharp cheddar blended with mozzarella gives sweet potatoes a great taste. Try these for breakfast, too!

Bake the sweet potatoes for 45 to 60 minutes in Dutch oven or 1 hour in a 350°F conventional oven. Set aside to cool.

Cut each sweet potato in half lengthwise and scoop out pulp. Mash with a fork and put in Dutch oven or 9″ × 12″ baking pan. Sprinkle cheddar cheese, mozzarella cheese, and raisins over potatoes.

Bake in Dutch oven for 3 to 5 minutes, or in 350°F conventional oven for 5 to 10 minutes, just long enough to melt cheeses. Top with Grape-Nuts cereal. Serve hot.

Yield: 6 servings

RICE PILAF WITH DRIED APRICOTS AND PINE NUTS

1 teaspoon olive oil
½ cup chopped onion
1½ cups arborio rice or medium-grain white
    rice
¼ cup chopped dried apricots
1 garlic clove, minced
3 cups chicken broth
¼ cup chopped tomato
salt and freshly ground black pepper to taste
2 tablespoons chopped cilantro
2 tablespoons pine nuts, toasted

Heat Dutch oven or large pot over medium-high heat and add oil. Add onion and sauté until golden, about 4 minutes. Add rice, apricots, and garlic; stir and cook 1 minute. Stir in chicken broth and tomato. Bring to boil.

Reduce heat to low, cover, and simmer until rice is tender and most of liquid is absorbed, about 25 minutes. Season with salt and pepper.

Transfer to bowl; sprinkle with cilantro and pine nuts and serve.

Yield: 4 servings as a side dish

TOMATO-BASIL-ONION TART

unsalted butter for greasing pan
1 sheet frozen puff pastry, thawed per
    directions
1 teaspoon unsalted butter
2 to 3 fresh tomatoes, sliced
1 sweet onion, thinly sliced
2 cups chopped fresh basil leaves
4 ounces fresh Parmesan cheese, grated
    (1 cup)
2 cloves garlic, minced
1 teaspoon salt
1 teaspoon black pepper
1 egg white
1 teaspoon water

Late in the summer season when your garden is producing delicious tomatoes and basil, this is a tasty, splashy way to indulge in them. It can be served as a meatless dinner with a fresh salad or as a side dish for grilled meat or fish. This recipe is for use in a conventional oven, but for a Dutch oven, double the recipe and it will make 8 to 10 servings.

Butter the bottom of a 12″ Dutch oven or 10″ tart pan. Roll out pastry sheet into a square that goes up the sides of the Dutch oven about 4 inches or overlaps the sides when placed in the tart pan.

Put on a layer of tomatoes, then onion and basil and sprinkle with a third of the Parmesan and half of the garlic, salt, and pepper. Repeat layer and top with remaining Parmesan.

Fold sides of puff pastry into the center loosely. Lightly beat egg white and water together. Brush egg wash on the pastry.

Bake about 45 minutes. For conventional oven, bake in 375°F oven for 45 minutes or until golden brown, puffed, and bubbling. Cool slightly before slicing

Yield: 4 to 8 servings

SAVORY BUTTERNUT SQUASH TART

1 small butternut squash (about 1 pound)
oil for brushing squash
pastry for 9-inch single-crust pie (see recipe
    on page 161)
flour for rolling out crust
1½ tablespoons unsalted butter, softened
2 large eggs
¼ cup whole milk
2 ounces Parmesan cheese, grated (½ cup)
3 teaspoons minced fresh sage
1 teaspoon granulated sugar
½ teaspoon salt
freshly ground black pepper to taste

Prior to making tart, prepare squash. Halve squash and scoop out seeds. Lightly brush each cut side with about 1 teaspoon oil and on a baking sheet roast squash, cut sides down, 12″ Dutch oven or in middle of oven 40 minutes, or until soft. Set aside to cool.

Roll out pie crust on lightly floured surface. Fit dough into a 12″ Dutch oven or 11″ tart pan. Place in Dutch oven and set aside.

Scoop out flesh of cooled squash and purée in food processor. Add butter, eggs, and milk and blend well. Transfer mixture to a large bowl and stir in cheese, sage, sugar, salt, and pepper. Pour filling into pie shell, smoothing top.

Bake in Dutch oven for 40 to 50 minutes. For conventional oven, bake at 375°F on the middle rack for 40 minutes, or until filling is set. Cool tart slightly before serving.

Yield: 6 to 8 servings

GRILLED SUMMER VEGETABLES WITH BROWN-BUTTER VINAIGRETTE

2 zucchini, quartered lengthwise
2 yellow squash, quartered lengthwise
1 red bell pepper, seeded, cut into strips
1 orange bell pepper, seeded, cut into strips
1 large onion, peeled and cut into 8 wedges
3 large tomatoes, thickly sliced
¼ cup olive oil
1 teaspoon kosher salt
½ teaspoon freshly ground black pepper
4 tablespoons unsalted butter
¼ cup red wine vinegar
¼ cup capers

This is a favorite summer recipe of friend Karen South in Montana.

Toss zucchini, squash, bell peppers, onion, and tomatoes with olive oil and season with salt and pepper. Grill on a grill screen over medium fire for 5 minutes per side.

Heat a Dutch oven or medium skillet over high heat and add butter. Cook until it begins to brown lightly. Remove from heat and stir in vinegar and capers.

Cut veggies in large bite-sized chunks, put in serving bowl and pour warm brown-butter vinaigrette over the top. Serve immediately.

Yield: 6 servings

EGGPLANT CURRY BY BRIAN AND KATIE REYNOLDS

1 cup uncooked brown rice
4 cups cold water
¼ to ½ cup olive oil
4 Japanese eggplants (long skinny ones), or
    2 regular eggplants (big fat ones), cut
    into bite-size cubes
1 medium-size yellow onion, coarsely
    chopped
1 cup uncooked white rice
1 zucchini, cut into bite-size cubes
1 can (13 ounces) coconut milk
3 fresh tomatoes, coarsely diced, or 1
    28-ounce can chopped tomatoes
1 to 2 tablespoons curry powder
salt and freshly ground black pepper to taste
plain yogurt
pinch of cayenne pepper

"This recipe is a great way to enjoy eggplant. We were told of this recipe by an old, burned-out, salty river guide who experimented with being a vegetarian for a summer. Each afternoon we would eagerly await his camp routine. He would row into camp after a long day of boating, tie off his boat, crack a beer, and say, 'Boys, booze is the duct tape of life!' and he would proceed to drink the whole can in one pull. Although he failed as a vegetarian, he succeeded in creating a fantastic recipe that the whole family can enjoy. Because our kids love this meal so much (use mild curry if there are kids), we now grow three different varieties of eggplant in our garden. Our two boys, Max and Owen, delight in tending and picking the purple fruit."

In a saucepan, add brown rice to water, stir, and begin heating on high (this way, the brown and white rice are ready at the same time).

In the meantime, heat a Dutch oven over medium-high heat and add oil. Sauté eggplants and onion. Eggplant soaks up olive oil quickly, so keep adding the oil until it appears saturated. Lots of olive oil is the key to tasty eggplant.

When water in saucepan with brown rice comes to a boil, add white rice. Stir and reduce heat to lowest setting. Cook for 20 minutes.

While rice simmers, continue to sauté eggplants and onion until translucent. Add zucchini and tomatoes and cook 3 minutes. Add coconut milk, curry powder, salt, and pepper and cook 5 minutes.

Serve the eggplant over rice with a dollop of yogurt and sprinkle of cayenne pepper.

Yield: 4 servings

NEW ZEALAND LEFTOVERS

8 new red potatoes
½ pound fresh mushrooms, sliced
2 tablespoons olive oil
1 pound asparagus, trimmed and halved
juice from 1 lime
½ cup crumbled blue or feta cheese
½ cup sun-dried tomatoes in oil, drained
   and chopped

Kathy Brower, a great friend from Pocatello, Idaho, shared this recipe with me. It comes from her cousin Kate McColl from Christchurch, New Zealand. "Kate is one of the most interesting and intriguing women. I met her back in 1971 while she was staying with my family and going to high school in North Dakota. This past December, after thirty-six years, Terry and I were fortunate enough to spend time with her while we toured New Zealand. Her home became our favorite place to come back to. She is a gifted teacher, writer, gardener, and cook. Having lived and taught in North Dakota and Colorado, she has an amusing outlook on the American way of life. She is a creative cook and has based most of her dishes on what was left in the fridge or what she found in the cupboard. One night she made this dish for us."

Boil potatoes until tender; cut into quarters.

Combine mushrooms and olive oil in Dutch oven or large skillet and sauté over medium-high heat until tender. Add potatoes, asparagus, and lime juice. Cook until asparagus is almost tender, about 3 to 4 minutes. Add half of the cheese and the sun-dried tomatoes, and stir to combine.

Remove from heat, place in a serving bowl, and toss with remaining cheese. Serve hot.

Yield: 6 servings

CUTTHROAT CRISPY POTATO CAKES

6 russet potatoes, peeled and coarsely
    grated
4 egg whites
2 shallots, finely minced
2 tablespoons minced garlic
½ tablespoon finely chopped fresh rosemary
1 teaspoon salt
½ teaspoon black pepper
cornmeal
peanut oil

This recipe is named for a species of trout found in the Middle Fork of the Salmon River.

Wrap grated potatoes in several layers of paper towels and squeeze dry. Place potatoes in large bowl. Add egg whites, shallots, garlic, rosemary, salt, and pepper, and toss to combine.

Using ½ cup of the mixture, pat into a cake, thoroughly coat with cornmeal on both sides. Heat oil on griddle, add potato cakes, and cook about 1½ minutes on each side until crisp and golden brown. Keep warm until ready to serve.

Yield: 6 servings

PEPPERS STUFFED WITH GOAT CHEESE

1 red pepper
1 yellow pepper
1 green pepper
6 tablespoons unsalted butter
1 cup finely chopped onions
1 garlic clove, minced
½ cup chopped chives
12 ounces goat cheese
2 teaspoons cumin seeds
¼ teaspoon cayenne pepper
salt and black pepper to taste
½ cup pine nuts

Serve this as a meal with salsa and French bread, or alone as an appetizer.

Slice tops off red, yellow, and green peppers. Remove ribs and seeds, but leave peppers whole.

Melt butter in skillet and sauté onions and garlic until translucent. Combine with chives, goat cheese, cumin seeds, cayenne pepper, salt, pepper, and pine nuts. Mix well. (You can also prepare this in a food processor before your camping trip. If you do so, add pine nuts at the end so they are not too finely ground.)

Stuff peppers with mixture and smooth tops with spatula. Chill for 3 hours. When stuffing is firm, cut each pepper into six slices, discarding bottoms. Put slices under broiler or in Dutch oven, stuffing-side up, with maximum heat on the top. Broil or heat until moisture begins to glaze the surface of the peppers. Serve one red, one green, and one yellow pepper slice for each serving.

Yield: 6 servings

Desserts

Remember

When a recipe calls for baking, braising, stewing, or roasting, the Dutch oven must be covered with charcoal briquettes on top of the lid. For boiling, frying, sautéing, and quick heating, leave the Dutch oven cover off. For more on cooking techniques for the Dutch oven, see "Dutch Oven Care and Use," pages 2–4. When using a conventional oven, preheat the oven to the given temperature.

GRANDMA'S APPLE CAKE

unsalted butter for greasing pan plus ½ cup, diced, at room temperature

1½ cups plus 2 tablespoons whole wheat flour

5 teaspoons cornstarch

2¼ teaspoons baking soda

¾ teaspoon salt

⅛ teaspoon ground cloves

4 medium Gala apples, peeled, cored, and cut into ⅓-inch slices

¾ cup, plus 1 tablespoon packed brown sugar

2 large eggs

2 tablespoons milk

2 teaspoons granulated sugar

2 tablespoons confectioners' sugar

Grease a Dutch oven or 9″ × 12″ baking pan and set aside.

Combine flour, cornstarch, baking soda, salt, and cloves. Cut in butter with pastry blender or fingers until mixture is the consistency of coarse cornmeal. Mix in apples and brown sugar.

In a separate bowl, whisk eggs and milk together. Stir into apple mixture to make a thick batter. Put into Dutch oven or pan and sprinkle with granulated sugar.

Bake in Dutch oven for about 35 minutes, or in 350°F conventional oven for 35 to 45 minutes, until golden and springy to the touch. Sprinkle top with confectioners' sugar.

Yield: 8 servings

APPLE CRISP

6 to 7 apples, chopped

½ cup brown sugar

½ cup granulated sugar

¾ cup unbleached all-purpose flour

1 teaspoon ground cinnamon

½ cup (1 stick) butter, melted

This recipe is from Keri O'Connor's mom. Keri, who prefers crisps without oatmeal, loves it.

Place chopped apples in buttered 12″inch Dutch oven or buttered 9″ × 13″ glass baking dish.

Combine sugars, flour, cinnamon, and melted butter. Spoon over apples.

Put Dutch oven on six coals and place twelve to fifteen on top. Bake 45 minutes. For conventional oven, bake at 350°F for 45 minutes or until golden brown.

Yield: 8 to 10 servings

ALPINE APPLE CRISP

5 medium-sized apples, cored, peeled, and sliced
¾ cup margarine, melted
¾ cup chopped walnuts
1½ cups rolled oats
1 teaspoon cinnamon
½ cup sunflower seeds
½ cup unbleached all-purpose flour
½ teaspoon allspice
¾ cup brown sugar
¾ cup orange juice
3 cups whipped cream, sweetened (optional)

Spread half of the apples in a 10" Dutch oven or 9" × 12" baking pan.

In a separate bowl, combine margarine with walnuts, oats, cinnamon, sunflower seeds, flour, allspice, and brown sugar. Crumble half of this mixture onto apples. Layer the remaining apples, and top with the rest of the topping. Pour orange juice over top.

Bake in Dutch oven for 45 minutes, or in 375°F conventional oven for 45 minutes, until the apples are soft. Top with whipped cream if desired.

Yield: 8 servings

SUE'S APPLE-RAISIN CRUMBLE

butter for greasing pan

Filling
6 large apples, peeled and sliced
½ cup raisins
½ cup honey
1 teaspoon ground cinnamon

Crumble Crust
1½ cups quick oats, uncooked
1 tablespoon sesame seeds
1 tablespoon wheat germ
¼ cup coconut
¼ cup sunflower seeds
½ cup margarine
½ cup honey

This recipe was given to me by my good friend Bill Caccia, who borrowed it from an Australian friend. He makes it in a Dutch oven on a cookstove at home, as well as over a campfire on float trips.

Grease a Dutch oven or 9" × 12" baking pan and set aside.

Mix apples, raisins, honey, and cinnamon. Place in Dutch oven or pan and set aside.

Make the crust: Mix oats, sesame seeds, wheat germ, coconut, and sunflower seeds. Cut in margarine and add enough honey to create a crumbly texture. Cover the apples and raisins with the crumble mixture.

Bake for 30 minutes in Dutch oven, or for 30 minutes in a 350°F conventional oven, until top is golden brown.

Yield: 8 servings

SUGARLESS APPLE TARTS

1 can (12 ounces) frozen apple juice
    concentrate
2 tablespoons unsalted butter plus more for
    greasing backs of muffin tins
3 tablespoons quick-cooking tapioca
⅛ teaspoon salt
1 teaspoon ground cinnamon
½ teaspoon ground nutmeg
6 to 7 cups peeled, thinly sliced Golden
    Delicious apples
pastry for a 9-inch double-crust pie (recipe
    on page 161)
flour for rolling out dough
3 cups whipped cream (optional),
    sweetened
½ cup chopped walnuts (optional)

In Dutch oven or saucepan, combine apple juice concentrate, butter, tapioca, salt, cinnamon, nutmeg, and apples. Simmer, covered and occasionally stirring gently, until apples are tender, about 10 to 15 minutes. Cool. Can be covered and chilled for up to four days.

Grease the back sides of twelve 2½-inch individual aluminum metal muffin cups.

Prepare pastry dough according to directions. On a floured board, roll out pastry to about ⅛ inch thick. Cut into twelve 4½-inch rounds. Drape pastry rounds over the backs of the greased muffin cups. Shape dough around each cup. Prick bottom of each round with fork.

Bake tart shells, bottom-side up, in Dutch oven for 5 to 7 minutes, or in 450°F conventional oven for 7 to 8 minutes, until golden brown. Let tart shells cool before removing from muffin cups.

Spoon about ⅓ cup of apple filling into each tart shell. Garnish each tart with sweetened whipped cream and chopped nuts, if desired.

Yield: 12 servings

APPLE-CHEDDAR DUMPLINGS

unsalted butter for greasing pan

Pastry

3 cups unbleached all-purpose flour

¼ cup granulated sugar

¾ teaspoon salt

4 tablespoons chilled unsalted butter, cut into pieces

¼ cup chilled vegetable shortening, cut into pieces

1¾ cups packed, finely grated, extra-sharp cheddar cheese

¾ cup ice water

Filling

4 cups peeled, cored, and thinly sliced Granny Smith apples

½ cup coarsely chopped walnuts

6 tablespoons brown sugar

1 teaspoon ground cinnamon

½ teaspoon nutmeg

3 tablespoons chilled unsalted butter, cut into pieces

Glaze

1 egg

1 tablespoon whipping cream

Topping

1 cup plain yogurt or sour cream

2 tablespoons maple syrup

Grease a Dutch oven or 9″ × 12″ baking pan and set aside.

Make the pastry: Combine flour, granulated sugar, and salt. Cut in butter and the shortening with a pastry blender or your fingers. Add cheese and continue to blend until mixture resembles coarse cornmeal. Mix in water until dough holds together. Knead dough briefly.

Make the filling: Combine apples, walnuts, brown sugar, cinnamon, and nutmeg. Set aside.

Make the glaze: Whip together the egg and cream. The glaze should be thick and creamy. Set aside.

Roll out dough to ¼-inch thickness. Cut into eight 3-inch squares. Place a scoop of apple filling in center of each square. Dot apple filling with 3 tablespoons chilled butter. Fold up the corners of each filled square, creating a package. Pinch edges to seal dough and brush top with glaze. Place in the bottom of Dutch oven or baking pan.

Bake in Dutch oven for about 40 minutes, or in 350°F conventional oven for 40 minutes, until crusts are golden brown.

Whisk yogurt, or sour cream, and syrup together and spoon over each serving.

Yield: 8 servings

DEVIL'S TOOTH CHEESECAKE

Crust

4 tablespoons unsalted butter, melted

1 package chocolate cookie wafers, crushed

Filling

16 ounces cream cheese, softened

1 cup sugar

16 ounces ricotta cheese

6 eggs, slightly beaten

½ cup sour cream

12 ounces semisweet chocolate chips

¼ cup unsalted butter

½ cup whipping cream

1½ teaspoons almond flavoring

1½ teaspoons vanilla extract

This dessert is served by Kurt and Gail Selisch of Middle Fork River Tours. It is named after Devil's Tooth Rapid.

Make the crust: Blend the butter with the cookie crumbs and press mixture into a 10″ Dutch oven or springform pan. Press the dough up the sides of pan at least 1 inch. Set aside.

Mix cream cheese, sugar, ricotta, eggs, and sour cream until smooth. Set aside.

Melt chocolate chips, butter, and whipping cream over low heat until smooth. Add almond flavoring. Pour one-third of the cheese mixture into chocolate mixture, and mix well. Pour this into crust. Add vanilla to remaining cheese mixture and carefully pour this over the chocolate layer.

Bake in Dutch oven or 350°F conventional oven for about 1¼ hours, or until the top cracks and the cake is firm. Serve warm or chilled.

Yield: 10 to 12 servings

APPLESAUCE CAKE

unsalted butter for greasing pan

1½ cups honey

½ cup margarine

2 eggs

2 teaspoons baking soda

2½ cups unbleached all-purpose flour

½ teaspoon allspice

1 teaspoon ground cinnamon

1½ cups applesauce

½ cup boiling water

Grease a Dutch oven or 9″ × 12″ baking pan and set aside.

Mix all ingredients except water in large bowl. Add water and mix well again. Pour into Dutch oven or baking pan.

Bake in Dutch oven for 45 to 50 minutes, or in 350°F conventional oven for 45 to 55 minutes.

Yield: 15 servings

CAMEL GULCH CARROT CAKE

unsalted butter for greasing pan
2 cups unbleached all-purpose flour
1½ teaspoons baking soda
2 teaspoons baking powder
1 teaspoon salt
2 teaspoons ground cinnamon
2 cups sugar
1½ cups vegetable oil
4 eggs
2 cups grated carrots
1 can (8 ounces) crushed pineapple,
    drained
1 cup flaked coconut
½ cup chopped walnuts

Camel Gulch is a drainage gulch on the Salmon River in Idaho. It is named for the Camel family, who lived at the mouth of the river in the days of Idaho's earliest settlers.

Lightly butter a 12″ Dutch oven or 9″ × 12″ baking pan.

In a large bowl combine flour, baking soda, baking powder, salt, and cinnamon. Stir in sugar, vegetable oil, eggs, carrots, pineapple, coconut, and walnuts. Pour batter into Dutch oven or pan.

Bake in Dutch oven for 30 to 40 minutes, or in 350°F conventional oven for 45 to 55 minutes. Let cool and frost with Cream Cheese Frosting (recipe follows).

Yield: 12 to 15 servings

CREAM CHEESE FROSTING

8 ounces cream cheese, softened
½ cup unsalted butter
1 teaspoon vanilla extract
⅓ cup confectioners' sugar

Combine cream cheese, butter, and vanilla; beat until fluffy. Gradually add the confectioners' sugar. Beat again until smooth.

APRICOT UPSIDE-DOWN SKILLET CAKE

3 tablespoons unsalted butter
⅓ cup plus ⅔ cup honey
2 cups halved fresh apricots
¼ cup chopped almonds
½ cup margarine or oil
2 eggs
1 teaspoon vanilla extract
½ teaspoon baking soda
¼ cup yogurt or buttermilk
1¾ cups whole wheat pastry flour
3 cups whipped cream, sweetened, or sour
    cream

Tawna Skinner, a Salmon River entrepreneur and organic gardener extraordinaire, shared this mouth-watering recipe with me.

Melt butter over low heat in bottom of heavy skillet or Dutch oven. Stir in ⅓ cup honey. Simmer until well mixed and slightly thickened. If cooking conventionally, pour mixture into 9″ × 9″ baking pan.

Arrange apricots, cut-side down, over mixture. Cover with almonds.

In large bowl, blend margarine or oil and remaining ⅔ cup honey. Beat in eggs one at a time until blended. Add vanilla.

In a small bowl, combine baking soda and yogurt or buttermilk. Add to egg mixture. Add flour and mix well. The batter should be rather thin. Pour batter over apricots.

Bake in Dutch oven over medium heat for 30 to 40 minutes, or in 250°F conventional oven for 40 to 50 minutes. Remove from pan immediately by inverting a large plate over skillet or Dutch oven and turning whole assembly upside down. Serve warm or cold topped with whipped cream or sour cream.

Yield: 8 to 10 servings

PASTRY CRUST FOR DOUBLE-CRUST PIE

2 cups unbleached all-purpose flour
1 teaspoon salt
⅔ cup shortening
5 to 7 tablespoons cold water

This recipe makes enough dough for an 8", 9", or 10" double-crust pie. For recipes requiring a single-crust pastry shell, simply cut these ingredients in half.

Mix flour and salt. Cut in shortening with pastry blender or fork until pieces are the size of small peas. Sprinkle water over mixture. Gently toss with a fork until moist.

Divide dough for top and bottom crusts and form into two balls. Flatten on lightly floured surface. Roll from center out to ⅛-inch thickness.

Fold dough into quarters and lift into Dutch oven or pie plate. Shape edges as desired. Proceed with pie recipe instructions.

(For single-crust pies requiring a prebaked crust, bake in Dutch oven for 10 to 12 minutes, or in 450°F conventional oven for 10 to 12 minutes.)

CHERRY PIE

pastry for a 10-inch double-crust pie (see preceding recipe)
3 cups tart, fresh red cherries, pitted
1 cup sugar
¼ cup unbleached all-purpose flour
dash salt
2 tablespoons unsalted butter, chilled and cut into pieces

Line the bottom of a 10" Dutch oven with prepared pastry shell, or place pie tin with pastry shell directly in the bottom of the Dutch oven. If baking conventionally, place prepared pastry shell in 10" pie dish.

Combine cherries, sugar, flour, and salt. Pour into pastry shell and dot with butter. Cover with second pastry shell and seal, crimping edges. Bake in Dutch oven for 40 to 45 minutes, or in 350°F conventional oven for 40 to 45 minutes. Let cool before slicing.

Yield: 8 servings

GLAZED PEACH PIE

pastry for a 10-inch single-crust pie (see recipe on page 161)
5 cups sliced fresh peaches
¾ cup fructose or granulated sugar
3 tablespoons unbleached all-purpose flour
½ teaspoon nutmeg
¼ teaspoon salt
1 teaspoon lemon juice
¼ teaspoon almond extract
¼ cup apricot preserves

Prepare pastry dough. Form it into a deep-dish crust in Dutch oven or pie tin (you may place metal pie tin inside Dutch oven). Preheat lid to Dutch oven or if using conventional oven, preheat to 425°F.

Toss together peaches, fructose or sugar, flour, nutmeg, salt, lemon juice, and almond extract. Arrange two circles of peach slices, all pointing to center, over the bottom of the crust. Top with two more layers of peach slices arranged in the same way.

Bake pie in Dutch oven or in 425°F conventional oven for 15 to 20 minutes; then cover with foil and bake 15 to 20 minutes longer until peaches are fork-tender.

Melt apricot preserves and brush over peaches.

Yield: 8 servings

BLACKBERRY COBBLER

Filling
⅔ cup sugar
2 tablespoons unbleached all-purpose flour
4 cups fresh or thawed frozen blackberries (16 ounces)

Crust
½ cup unbleached all-purpose flour
1 teaspoon baking powder
½ cup whole wheat flour
1½ tablespoons unsalted butter or margarine, chilled
6 tablespoons milk
flour for rolling out dough

Make the filling: Combine sugar and 2 tablespoons flour. Add blackberries. Pour into a 10″ Dutch oven or 9″ × 9″ baking dish, and set aside.

Make the crust: Mix ½ cup flour, baking powder, and whole wheat flour. Cut in butter or margarine with pastry blender or fingers until mixture resembles coarse crumbs. Stir in milk to make a soft dough and knead lightly until smooth. Put dough on a floured board and roll out to an 11-inch circle.

Place dough over berries, trimming to fit. Cut slits in dough for steam to escape.

Bake in Dutch oven for 20 to 30 minutes, or in 350°F conventional oven for 25 to 35 minutes, until crust is browned and filling is bubbly.

Yield: 6 servings

BAKED BLACKBERRY ROLLUPS

¼ cup unsalted butter, melted, plus ¼ cup
    chilled
1 cup water
1 cup plus 3 tablespoons sugar
1½ cups self-rising cake flour
⅓ cup milk
flour for rolling out dough
½ teaspoon ground cinnamon
3 cups fresh or thawed frozen blackberries

Line a 10″ Dutch oven or 9″ × 9″ baking pan with parchment paper.

In a saucepan, combine melted butter, water, and 1 cup of the sugar and heat until sugar is dissolved.

Cut chilled butter into flour with pastry blender or fingers until it resembles coarse cornmeal. Add milk and stir just until dough forms. Put dough on a floured board and roll out into an 11″ × 9″ rectangle. Sprinkle dough with cinnamon and scatter blackberries over the top.

Beginning at the long side, roll dough up jelly-roll fashion. Cut rolled dough into 1½-inch slices. Arrange slices (they will be messy), cut-side up, in Dutch oven or pan. Pour sugar syrup over slices.

Bake for 40 minutes in Dutch oven or 350°F conventional oven. Sprinkle 3 tablespoons sugar over the top and bake 15 more minutes or until golden brown.

Yield: 6 servings

COCONUT CAKE

2 large eggs, lightly beaten
¾ cup water
1 box white cake mix
1 can (6–8 ounces) coconut milk
1 can (12 ounces) condensed milk
8 ounces whipped topping
1 cup shredded coconut

Amie Bruggmans's so easy but good cake.

Combine the eggs and water. Add the cake mix and stir just until mixed. Bake in a 12″ Dutch oven for 35 to 40 minutes, or in a 9″ × 13″ pan at 325°F for 40 to 45 minutes.

With the handle of a wooden spoon, poke holes in warm cake. Combine coconut milk and condensed milk. Pour mixture over cake, filling holes. Cool.

Frost cake with whipped topping and sprinkle with coconut. Chill.

Yield: 10 servings

STRAWBERRY-YOGURT CHEESECAKE

Crust

8 tablespoons margarine, melted
¼ cup honey
2 cups graham crackers, crushed

Filling

8 ounces cream cheese, softened
2 teaspoons vanilla extract
2 cups plain yogurt
¼ cup honey
¼ teaspoon salt
2 eggs
1 quart fresh strawberries, sliced

Prepare the crust: Stir margarine and honey together and mix with crackers. Press crust firmly into 10″ metal pie tin (or you can use a glass pan if baking this in a conventional oven). If making in Dutch oven, place pie tin inside Dutch oven.

Beat cream cheese with vanilla until creamy. Add the yogurt, honey, and salt, and mix well. Add eggs one at a time, mixing just until blended. Pour mixture into shell.

Bake in Dutch oven or in 350°F conventional oven for about 1 hour, until firm.

Let cool and top with sliced strawberries. Chill at least 1 hour before serving.

Yield: 8 servings

PEACH CRUMB FLAN

Crust

6 tablespoons unsalted butter
1 cup whole wheat flour
¼ cup honey

Filling

8 ounces Neufchâtel or light cream cheese, softened
2 tablespoons plus 4 tablespoons honey
1 egg
½ teaspoon vanilla extract
4 cups sliced, peeled fresh peaches (or use canned peaches, drained)
½ teaspoon cinnamon
¼ cup sliced almonds

Make the crust: Cut the butter into the flour. Add ¼ cup honey, and mix. Pat the mixture into the bottom of a Dutch oven or 9″ × 12″ baking pan, extending the crust 1½ inches up the sides. Bake crust in Dutch oven or in 350°F conventional oven for 8 to 10 minutes.

Make the filling: Mix the Neufchâtel or cream cheese and 2 tablespoons of the honey until smooth. Add egg and vanilla, and blend well. Pour filling into crust.

In a separate bowl, toss the peaches with the remaining 4 tablespoons honey and cinnamon until evenly coated. Spoon peaches onto cream cheese mixture. Sprinkle almonds on top.

Bake in Dutch oven for 25 to 35 minutes, or in 350°F conventional oven for 30 to 35 minutes, or until the almonds are lightly toasted.

Yield: 8 servings

unsalted butter for greasing pan (unless using parchment)

Filling

7½ cups frozen blueberries (16 ounces)
7 cups peeled, chopped Granny Smith apples
2 teaspoons lemon zest
1 tablespoon fresh lemon juice
½ cup unbleached all-purpose flour
¾ cup granulated sugar
⅓ cup packed brown sugar
1¾ teaspoons ground cinnamon

Topping

1 cup quick-cooking oats
⅓ cup unbleached all-purpose flour
¾ cup packed brown sugar
pinch salt
2 tablespoons chilled unsalted butter, cut into pieces
2 tablespoons canola oil

BLUEBERRY-APPLE CRUMBLE

Impress your friends with this colorful, delicious dessert.

Butter a Dutch oven or 9″ × 12″ baking pan, or line with parchment paper, extending paper 2 inches up sides.

Make the filling: Combine blueberries, apples, lemon zest, and lemon juice. In a separate bowl, stir together flour, sugars, and cinnamon. Stir the two mixtures together and place in Dutch oven or pan. Bake in Dutch oven or 350°F conventional oven for 20 minutes.

Make the topping: Combine oats, flour, brown sugar, and salt. Cut in 2 tablespoons butter with a pastry blender or with fingers. Stir in oil. Sprinkle topping evenly over fruit.

Bake for 30 to 40 more minutes, until top is brown and fruit is bubbly.

Yield: 16 servings

RASPBERRY BREAD PUDDING

unsalted butter for greasing pan

Pudding

2 cups milk
½ cup granulated sugar
¼ teaspoon nutmeg
1 teaspoon vanilla extract
3 eggs, lightly beaten
3 cups day-old Italian or French bread, cut
    in 1-inch cubes
4 tablespoons unsalted butter, melted
1 cup raspberries, fresh or frozen
1 tablespoon confectioners' sugar

Raspberry Sauce

1 cup raspberries, fresh or frozen
2 tablespoons confectioners' sugar
3 cups whipped cream, sweetened (optional)

Grease a Dutch oven or 9″ × 12″ baking pan and set aside.

Bring milk just to a boil, remove from heat, and stir in granulated sugar. Add nutmeg and vanilla and let cool for 10 minutes. Whisk in eggs.

In a separate bowl, toss bread cubes with melted butter. Pour bread mixture into Dutch oven or pan and spoon berries over top. Pour milk-and-egg mixture over bread mixture.

Bake in Dutch oven or in 350°F conventional oven for 1 hour, until set and starting to brown. Let cool. Dust with 1 tablespoon confectioners' sugar.

Make raspberry sauce: Push the remaining 1 cup raspberries through a sieve. Mix resulting juice with 2 tablespoons confectioners' sugar. Cook over medium heat, stirring until sugar is completely dissolved. Pour sauce over the cake and serve cake with whipped cream.

Yield: 6 servings

DELIGHTFUL PEACHES

6 medium peaches, pitted and cut into
    eighths
¼ cup orange juice concentrate
1½ cup crushed amaretti cookies (Italian
    macaroons), or almond macaroons
½ cup finely chopped toasted almonds
1 tablespoon unsweetened cocoa powder
¼ cup chilled unsalted butter, sliced
3 cups whipped cream, sweetened, or
    vanilla ice cream (optional)

Arrange peaches in a 10″ Dutch oven or 9″ × 9″ baking dish. Pour orange juice concentrate over peaches and toss gently. Let peach mixture stand for 30 minutes.

Combine cookies, almonds, and cocoa powder in small bowl. Add butter and rub mixture with fingertips until mixture resembles coarse cornmeal. Sprinkle over peaches.

Bake in Dutch oven for about 20 minutes, or in 350°F conventional oven for 20 to 25 minutes, until peaches are tender and topping is brown. Cool slightly. Serve with whipped cream or vanilla ice cream.

Yield: 6 servings

PEAR-CRANBERRY COBBLER

Crust

2½ cups unbleached all-purpose flour plus more for rolling out dough

1 teaspoon salt

10 tablespoons unsalted butter plus more for greasing pan

⅔ cup chilled vegetable shortening

½ cup ice water

Filling

7 cups cranberries (24 ounces)

8 pears, peeled and sliced

1 cup sugar

½ cup unbleached all-purpose flour

½ teaspoon ground allspice

¼ teaspoon ground cardamom

6 cups ice cream or whipped cream, sweetened (optional)

This is a simple but absolutely delicious Dutch oven dessert.

Butter a 12″ Dutch oven or 9″ × 12″ baking pan.

Make the crust: Mix 2½ cups flour and salt. Cut butter and shortening into flour with pastry blender or fingers until it forms pea-sized lumps. Add water, working mixture as little as possible until dough is formed. Wrap dough in plastic and chill for 20 minutes.

Sprinkle cranberries and pears with sugar, ½ cup flour, allspice, and cardamom. Mix well. Spread mixture in Dutch oven or pan. Put pastry on a floured board and roll out to ⅛-inch thickness, in a round 1 inch larger than pan.

Fold dough in half to place on top of fruit. Unfold carefully and crimp edges decoratively. Cut slits in top.

Bake in Dutch oven for 35 to 40 minutes, or in 350°F conventional oven for 50 to 60 minutes, until crust is golden brown and bubbly and cranberries have split. Cool 15 minutes and serve with ice cream or whipped cream.

Yield: 12 servings

FRUIT CRUMBLE

Filling

6 cups peeled and cored apples, chopped
    into ½- to ¾-inch pieces (about 6 large
    apples)

2 tablespoons sugar

½ teaspoon ground cinnamon

2 teaspoons fresh lemon juice

Topping

¾ cup unbleached all-purpose flour

½ cup sugar

½ teaspoon salt

½ cup (1 stick) cold unsalted butter, cut into
    ¾-inch pieces

vanilla ice cream (optional)

Prepare the filling: Put the apples in a 12″ Dutch oven or 2½-quart glass or ceramic baking dish. Mix the sugar and cinnamon together in a small bowl. Sprinkle the sugar mixture and lemon juice over the apples. Stir the mixture to combine the ingredients, spreading them in an even layer in Dutch oven or baking dish. Set aside.

Prepare the topping: Combine flour, sugar, and salt in a large bowl. Cut in the butter until coarse crumbs form and the mixture looks pale yellow rather than white. Spread the crumbs evenly over the apple mixture.

Bake about 40 minutes until the crumb topping is golden with a few spots of light brown and the apples are tender when tested with a toothpick. For conventional oven, bake on the center rack at 350°F for 45 minutes.

Let the crumble cool about 15 minutes before serving. Spoon the warm crumble onto individual plates and serve with a scoop of vanilla ice cream, if desired. The crumble can be baked a day ahead, cooled, covered, and stored at room temperature.

Yield: 6 servings

REDSIDE RHUBARB

3 cups diced rhubarb (preferably strawberry
    rhubarb, a sweet red variety)
2 tablespoons orange juice
⅓ cup plus ¼ cup honey
1 tablespoon unsalted butter
1 egg, beaten
1 teaspoon vanilla extract
2 tablespoons sour cream
1 cup pastry flour
¼ teaspoon salt
½ teaspoon baking soda

*"Redside" is both another name for cutthroat trout and the name
of a rapid on the Middle Fork of the Salmon River.*

Line a 10″ Dutch oven or 9″ × 9″ baking pan with parchment
paper, extending paper 2 inches up sides. Arrange rhubarb on
paper.

    In a small bowl, mix orange juice and ⅓ cup honey. Drizzle
over rhubarb. Dot with butter.

    In another bowl, combine egg, ¼ cup honey, vanilla, and sour
cream. In a separate bowl, mix flour, salt, and baking soda; add to
egg mixture. Spread resulting batter over rhubarb.

    Bake in Dutch oven for about 30 minutes, or in 350°F
conventional oven for 30 minutes, until browned.

Yield: 6 servings

RUBY RAPID RHUBARB PIE

Crust
1 cup unbleached all-purpose flour
⅓ cup confectioners' sugar
½ cup margarine

Filling
2 eggs, beaten
1½ cups granulated sugar
¼ cup unbleached all-purpose flour
¾ teaspoon salt
2 cups finely chopped rhubarb

*This is a recipe from my mother, Jane McDonald, which I adapted
for a Dutch oven and renamed on the Main Salmon River.*

Make the crust: Mix 1 cup flour, confectioners' sugar, and
margarine. Press into the bottom of Dutch oven or 9″ × 12″
baking pan. Bake in Dutch oven or in 375°F conventional oven
for 15 minutes, being careful not to burn the bottom.

    Mix eggs, sugar, ¼ cup flour, salt, and rhubarb. Spread
rhubarb mixture on top of the crust.

    Bake in Dutch oven for 30 minutes, or in 350°F conventional
oven for 30 minutes. Let stand 15 minutes before serving.

Yield: 8 to 10 servings

SOUR CREAM–RAISIN PIE

Crust

1 cup unbleached all-purpose flour, or
   ¾ cup whole wheat flour, plus more
   for rolling out dough
dash of salt
½ cup shortening
¼ cup water

Filling

½ cup plus ¼ cup water
1½ cups raisins
2 eggs
2 cups sour cream
1 teaspoon lemon juice or vinegar
pinch of salt
¾ cup sugar
2 tablespoons cornstarch
¼ cup water

My sister-in-law Angie Mills Cockran uses her grandmother's "no-fail" pie crust for this special dessert.

Make the crust: Mix flour and salt and cut in shortening with pastry blender or fingers. Add ¼ cup water and blend until a dough is formed. Roll out on floured board, put in Dutch oven or pie plate, and trim and crimp edges. Chill for 15 minutes.

Bake crust in Dutch oven or in 450°F conventional oven for 10 to 15 minutes, until brown.

Heat ½ cup water to boiling, pour over raisins, and let stand 5 minutes until raisins are plump.

Beat eggs and add sour cream, lemon juice or vinegar, salt, and sugar. Add to raisin mixture. Mix cornstarch with ¼ cup water and add to mixture. Cook over medium heat until it boils. Pour into prebaked pie shell. Let cool.

Yield: 6 servings

LEMON BARS

½ cup (1 stick) unsalted butter, melted
½ cup plus 2 tablespoons unbleached all-purpose flour
1¼ cups granulated sugar
½ teaspoon baking powder
2 eggs, beaten
2 tablespoons lemon juice
2 tablespoons additional lemon juice (optional)
¼ cup confectioners' sugar (optional)

My mother's good friend Martha Kraus, from Sun City, shared this delightfully rich dessert with her.

Mix butter, ½ cup flour, and sugar. Pat into a 10″ Dutch oven or 8″ × 8″ baking pan. Bake in Dutch oven or 350°F conventional oven for 15 minutes.

Mix remaining 2 tablespoons flour, baking powder, eggs, and lemon juice and pour over the crust.

Bake in Dutch oven or 350°F conventional oven for 25 minutes. Do not brown the top.

If desired, make a glaze of 2 tablespoons lemon juice and ¼ cup confectioners' sugar, and frost bars while warm. Or sprinkle with confectioners' sugar. Cool and cut into squares.

Yield: 12 bars

DOUBLE CHOCOLATE BROWNIES

4 ounces unsweetened chocolate
1 cup (2 sticks) unsalted butter plus more for greasing pan
1½ cups granulated sugar
4 eggs
2 teaspoons vanilla extract
1 cup unbleached all-purpose flour
pinch salt
12 ounces chocolate chips
2 cups miniature marshmallows
confectioners' sugar

Melt chocolate over low heat. Add sugar and butter and stir until sugar dissolves. Cool. Mix in eggs, vanilla, flour, salt, chocolate chips, and marshmallows well.

Butter a 12″ Dutch oven or line with parchment paper and bake 25 to 30 minutes. For conventional oven, butter 9″ × 13″ pan and bake at 350°F for 30 to 35 or until knife inserted into center comes out clean. Sprinkle confectioners' sugar on top when done. Cool and cut into squares.

Yield: 12 servings

RHUBARB CAKE

unsalted butter for greasing pan, plus
    2 tablespoons
½ cup margarine
1½ cups brown sugar, or 1 cup honey
2 eggs
1 teaspoon baking soda
1 cup sour cream
2 cups sifted flour, unbleached all-purpose
    or whole wheat
1½ cups diced rhubarb
1 teaspoon vanilla extract
½ cup chopped nuts
½ cup granulated sugar
1 teaspoon cinnamon

Grease a 9" × 13" pan or 12" Dutch oven and set aside.

Cream margarine and brown sugar or honey. Add eggs and blend well.

In a separate bowl, combine baking soda and sour cream. Add to creamed mixture alternately with flour and blend well. Add rhubarb, vanilla, and nuts. Pour batter into pan.

In a small bowl, blend granulated sugar, cinnamon, and butter. Sprinkle on top of batter.

Bake in Dutch oven for 30 to 40 minutes, or in 350°F conventional oven for 30 to 40 minutes.

Yield: 10 to 12 servings

UNBEATABLE PECAN BROWNIES

unsalted butter for greasing pan
4 ounces unsweetened chocolate
¼ cup plus ¾ cup plus 2 tablespoons
    unsalted butter, softened
1¾ cups sugar
3 large eggs
1 cup chopped pecans, lightly toasted
2½ tablespoons sour cream
pinch ground cinnamon
1 cup unbleached all-purpose flour, sifted

Butter a 12" Dutch oven or 9" × 13" pan.

Melt chocolate and ¼ cup butter over low heat, stirring until smooth. Let cool completely.

Cream remaining butter and sugar; beat until light and fluffy. Add eggs, one at a time, beating well after each. Beat in chocolate-butter mixture. Stir in pecans, sour cream, cinnamon, and flour. Pour the batter into Dutch oven or pan, smoothing the top with a spatula or knife.

Bake in Dutch oven for 30 to 40 minutes, or in 350°F conventional oven for 30 to 40 minutes, until batter pulls away from the sides of the pan slightly and a wooden pick inserted in the center comes out with crumbs clinging to it. Let cake cool before cutting.

Yield: 24 brownies

CORNY LEMON CAKE

yellow cornmeal for dusting parchment
1 cup yellow cornmeal
½ cup unbleached all-purpose flour
1½ teaspoons baking powder
¼ teaspoon salt
1 cup sugar
¼ cup canola oil
2 tablespoons butter, softened
2 large eggs
2 egg whites
½ cup plain yogurt
1½ tablespoons lemon zest
1 tablespoon fresh lemon juice
½ teaspoon lemon extract
1 cup assorted fresh or frozen thawed
    berries
¼ cup crème de cassis liqueur

Line a Dutch oven or 9″ × 12″ baking pan with parchment paper, extending paper 2 inches up sides. Dust with cornmeal and set aside.

Mix together 1 cup cornmeal, flour, baking powder, and salt, and set aside.

In a separate bowl, whisk together sugar, oil, and butter until well combined. Add eggs and egg whites, one at a time, until blended.

In a small bowl, stir together yogurt, lemon zest, lemon juice, and lemon extract. Fold into sugar-egg mixture until just combined. Fold lemon mixture into dry ingredients until just combined. Do not overmix. Pour batter into Dutch oven or pan and smooth the top with a spatula or knife.

Bake in Dutch oven for about 40 minutes, or in 350°F conventional oven for 40 to 45 minutes, until toothpick inserted in center comes out clean.

Toss berries with liqueur. Cut cake into wedges and serve, topped with berries.

Yield: 12 servings

WAR CAKE

unsalted butter for greasing pan
flour for dusting pan
2 cups water
2 cups sugar
1 cup shortening
2 cups raisins
1 cup walnuts (optional)
½ teaspoon ground cloves
1 teaspoon ground cinnamon
2 cups unbleached all-purpose flour
¼ teaspoon allspice
2 teaspoons baking soda

My sister-in-law Angie Mills Cochran's mother made this cake during World War II when groceries were in short supply. She called it "eggless, butterless, milkless cake."

Grease and flour a Dutch oven or 9" × 12" cake pan and set aside.

Combine water, sugar, shortening, raisins, walnuts (if desired), cloves, and cinnamon in a saucepan. Bring to a boil and cool. Add enough flour to stiffen mixture. Add allspice and baking soda.

Bake in Dutch oven for 30 minutes, or in 325°F conventional oven for 30 minutes, until center springs back when touched.

Yield: 12 servings

ELVERA'S SOURDOUGH CHOCOLATE CAKE

½ cup Sourdough Starter (see recipe on page 56)
1 cup warm water
1½ cups unbleached all-purpose flour
¼ cup powdered milk
butter for greasing pans
1 cup sugar
½ cup vegetable shortening
½ teaspoon salt
1½ teaspoons baking soda
1 teaspoon ground cinnamon
1 teaspoon vanilla extract
2 eggs
3 ounces unsweetened chocolate

Mix starter, warm water, flour, and powdered milk and let ferment 2 to 3 hours in a warm place until mixture is bubbly and smells sour.

Grease a 10" Dutch oven or two round layer pans.

Cream sugar, shortening, salt, soda, cinnamon, and vanilla thoroughly. Add eggs one at a time, beating well after each addition.

Melt chocolate over low heat. Combine creamed mixture and melted chocolate with sourdough mixture. Stir 300 strokes by hand or in mixer on low speed until blended. Pour into Dutch oven or two layer pans.

Bake in Dutch oven for 25 to 30 minutes, or in 350°F conventional oven for 25 to 30 minutes. Cool before frosting with your favorite icing.

Yield: 12 servings

IMPOSSIBLY POSSIBLE DUTCH-OVEN ICE CREAM

1 small package (3.4 ounces) instant
    pudding (any flavor)
2 cups milk
½ cup sugar
1 egg
½ tablespoon vanilla extract
¼ teaspoon lemon juice
1 cup whipping cream
1 can (12 ounces) evaporated milk

Neil and Carrie Dabb submitted this winner at the World Championship Dutch Oven Cookoff in Logan, Utah.

Chill a 12″ Dutch oven in a cooler or refrigerator.

Mix pudding and milk. In a separate bowl, mix sugar, egg, vanilla, and lemon juice. Add to pudding mixture.

Pour mixture into a dry and very cool Dutch oven. Add whipping cream and evaporated milk; stir. Put lid on Dutch oven. Place oven in a 16″ bowl. Arrange crushed ice and rock salt around oven as you would in an ice-cream freezer (alternating 1-inch layers of ice and ¼-inch to ½-inch layers of salt). Placing ice on the lid (no deeper than the lip) will cool the oven down faster.

Lift the lid and stir every 2 to 5 minutes. It will go slowly at first until the oven cools off. Add ice and salt to bowl as needed. Total freezing time is 30 to 45 minutes. The ice cream may be eaten soft, or if you prefer harder ice cream, you may replace the lid and cover it with ice and salt.

Note: Any ice-cream recipe may be frozen with this method; however, a cooked ice cream may pick up a unique flavor from the cast iron of the oven. If a cooked recipe is used, make sure the oven is well cooled before placing it in the ice (a hot oven could crack or shatter if placed directly in the ice).

Yield: 8 to 10 servings

GRANDMA SLAVIN'S BROWNIES

Brownies
½ cup (1 stick) unsalted butter
2 ounces unsweetened chocolate
1 cup sugar
1 cup sifted unbleached all-purpose flour
2 eggs
1 teaspoon vanilla extract
½ cup chopped walnuts

Frosting
¼ cup milk
1 ounce unsweetened chocolate
2 tablespoons unsalted butter
2 cups confectioners' sugar
1 teaspoon vanilla extract

River guide Chace Slavin shared his grandmother's recipe with us. This recipe is for using a conventional oven. When using a Dutch oven, double the ingredients.

Prepare brownies: Melt butter and chocolate together over low heat. Stir in sugar and flour. Add eggs and vanilla extract, mixing until just blended. Fold in walnuts. Pour mixture in 12″ Dutch oven. Bake 15 minutes. For conventional oven, bake in greased 8-inch square pan at 375°F for 15 to 20 minutes, until knife inserted into center comes out clean.

Prepare frosting: Bring the milk to a simmer and add the remaining ingredients, stirring until melted and well combined. Spread on cooled brownies.

Yield: 8 to 10 servings

APRICOT-RAISIN BARS

unsalted butter for greasing pan

Filling
½ cup dried apricots, diced
¼ cup raisins
½ cup apples, peeled and grated
½ cup apricot preserves

Crust
1½ teaspoons baking soda
1 cup unbleached all-purpose flour
½ cup oat bran
2 cups rolled oats
1 teaspoon ground cinnamon
1 cup brown sugar
¾ cup margarine, melted

Grease a 12″ Dutch oven or 9″ × 12″ baking pan and set aside.

Make the filling: In a medium-sized bowl, combine apricots, raisins, apples, and apricot preserves. Stir well and set aside.

Make the crust: In a large bowl, combine baking soda, flour, oat bran, oats, cinnamon, and brown sugar. Stir in melted margarine.

Press slightly more than half of crust mixture in bottom of Dutch oven or pan. Spread filling mixture over crust. Sprinkle remaining crust on top.

Bake in Dutch oven for 20 minutes, or in 350°F conventional oven for 20 to 25 minutes.

Yield: 24 bars

OATMEAL CAKE

Cake

unsalted butter for greasing pan
flour for dusting pan
1¼ cups boiling water
1 cup rolled oats
1 cup granulated sugar
1 cup brown sugar
½ cup (1 stick) unsalted butter or margarine
2 eggs
1⅓ cups unbleached all-purpose flour
1 teaspoon baking soda
½ teaspoon ground cinnamon
½ teaspoon salt
1 teaspoon vanilla extract

Topping

1 cup brown sugar
3 tablespoons unsalted butter, melted
6 tablespoons whipping cream
1 cup shredded coconut
1 cup chopped nuts

My mother often baked this moist and yummy cake when I was growing up.

Grease and flour a 12″ Dutch oven or 9″ × 13″ pan and set aside.

Pour boiling water over oats and let stand while mixing the rest of the cake.

Cream together sugars and butter or margarine. Add eggs and mix well.

In a separate bowl, sift together flour, baking soda, cinnamon, and salt. Add to sugar mixture. Stir in oatmeal mixture and vanilla. Pour batter into Dutch oven or pan.

Bake in Dutch oven for 30 minutes, or in 350°F conventional oven for 30 to 40 minutes.

Make the topping: Mix brown sugar, melted butter, cream, coconut, and nuts. Pour topping over partly cooled cake and place under broiler for a few minutes until brown and bubbly.

Yield: 12 servings

PEAR CRUMBLE

Filling

3 pounds firm ripe pears, peeled, cored, cut
  into ¼-inch slices
2 tablespoons fresh lemon juice
⅓ cup light brown sugar
2 tablespoons minced crystallized ginger
1½ tablespoons unbleached all-purpose
  flour

Topping

1½ cups unbleached all-purpose flour
½ cup granulated sugar
½ cup light brown sugar
1 teaspoon salt
1 cup (2 sticks) cold unsalted butter, cut into
  ¾-inch pieces
vanilla ice cream or whipped cream,
  sweetened (optional)

Mary Papale owns Idaho River Journeys with her husband, Bob Volpert. They are outfitters on the Middle Fork of the Salmon, Main Salmon, and the Rogue rivers. Mary is a great cook!

Prepare filling: Combine the pear slices and lemon juice in a large bowl. Add sugar, ginger, and flour and toss to blend. Place mixture in 12″ Dutch oven or buttered 9″ × 13″ glass baking dish.

Make topping: Combine flour, sugars, and salt in a large bowl. Cut in butter until coarse crumbs form and the mixture looks pale yellow rather than white. Spread the crumbs evenly over the pear mixture.

Bake about 40 minutes until the crumb topping is golden but with a few spots of light brown, and the pears are tender when tested with a toothpick. For conventional oven, bake at 350°F for 40 to 45 minutes. Let cool about 15 minutes before serving.

Crumble can be served with vanilla ice cream or whipped cream. The crumble can be baked a day ahead, cooled, covered, and stored at room temperature. Warm it, uncovered, in a preheated 250°F oven for 15 minutes.

Yield: 10 to 12 servings

YOGURT CHOCOLATE CAKE

unsalted butter for greasing pan
flour for dusting pan
1 egg, lightly beaten
⅔ cup plus 1 cup sugar
½ cup milk
3 ounces unsweetened chocolate
½ cup shortening
1 teaspoon vanilla extract
2 eggs
2 cups cake flour
1 teaspoon baking soda
½ teaspoon salt
1 cup plain or fruit yogurt
confectioners' sugar (optional)

Grease and flour a Dutch oven or 9″ × 12″ cake pan and set aside.

In a saucepan, combine egg, ⅔ cup sugar, milk, and unsweetened chocolate. Cook, stirring, over medium heat until chocolate melts and mixture just begins to boil. Set aside to cool.

In a separate bowl, cream 1 cup sugar and shortening until light and fluffy. Add vanilla. Add eggs, one at a time, beating well after each.

In a separate bowl, sift together cake flour, baking soda, and salt. Add flour mixture to creamed mixture alternately with yogurt, beating after each addition. Blend in chocolate mixture. Pour into Dutch oven or cake pan.

Bake in Dutch oven for 20 to 25 minutes, or in 350°F conventional oven for 25 to 30 minutes. Let cool, and frost with your favorite frosting or sprinkle with confectioners' sugar.

Yield: 12 servings

STREUSELY BAKED APPLES

12 pitted dates
3 large apples, cored and cut in half
½ cup sugar
½ cup unbleached all-purpose flour
¼ teaspoon ground cinnamon
¼ teaspoon ground cardamom
3 tablespoons unsalted butter
1 cup light cream

Line a Dutch oven or 9″ × 12″ baking pan with parchment paper, extending paper 2 inches up sides.

Place 2 dates in the hollow of each apple half.

Stir together the sugar, flour, cinnamon, and cardamom. Add butter and blend mixture with your fingers or a pastry blender. Using your fingers, pack mixture tightly in a mound over date-filled side of each apple half. Place apples, filling-side up, in Dutch oven or pan.

Bake in Dutch oven for 15 to 20 minutes, or in 350°F oven for 30 minutes, until apples are tender. Pass light cream to serve with fruit.

Yield: 3 to 6 servings

GINGERBREAD CAKE

¼ cup granulated sugar
½ cup milk
¼ cup molasses
¼ cup melted margarine
2 tablespoons honey
1 egg white
1 cup unbleached all-purpose flour
1 teaspoon ground ginger
1 teaspoon ground cinnamon
¾ teaspoon baking soda
¼ teaspoon salt
¼ teaspoon ground cloves
1 tablespoon confectioners' sugar
3 cups whipped cream or ice cream
    (optional)

Line a 10″ Dutch oven or 9″ × 9″ baking pan with parchment paper, extending paper 2 inches up sides.

Combine granulated sugar, milk, molasses, margarine, honey, and egg white, and beat until smooth. Set aside.

In a separate bowl, combine flour, ginger, cinnamon, baking soda, salt, and cloves. Stir well. Mix wet and dry mixtures together, beating well. Pour batter into Dutch oven or pan.

Bake in Dutch oven for 25 minutes, or in 350°F conventional oven for 25 to 35 minutes, until toothpick inserted in center comes out clean. Sprinkle with confectioners' sugar. Can be served with whipped cream or ice cream.

Yield: 6 servings

RHUBARB DUMPLINGS

Dough

2 cups unbleached all-purpose flour

2 tablespoons sugar

2 teaspoons baking powder

¼ teaspoon salt

2½ tablespoons chilled butter plus more for greasing pan

¾ cup milk

Filling

2 cups finely chopped rhubarb

½ cup sugar

½ teaspoon ground cinnamon

Topping

1 tablespoon all-purpose flour

½ teaspoon ground cinnamon

¼ teaspoon salt

1½ cups water

4 tablespoons unsalted butter

1 tablespoon vanilla extract

This delicious recipe was given to me by my good friend Beverly Ricks. In the small town of Salmon, Idaho, where she lives, most homes have a rhubarb plant in the yard.

Prepare dough: Combine flour, sugar, baking powder, and salt. Cut in butter until coarse crumbs form. Stir in milk until dough comes together into a ball. Chill for 30 minutes.

Prepare filling: Combine filling ingredients.

Roll out dough into a 6″ × 12″ rectangle. Spread the filling on top of dough. Roll up lengthwise and slice into 1½-inch pieces. Place onto buttered Dutch oven or cookie sheet.

Prepare topping: Place flour, cinnamon, salt, water, and butter in saucepan and bring to boil over medium-high heat. Boil 2 minutes until slightly thickened. Add vanilla. Pour over dumplings.

Bake 40 to 45 minutes in Dutch oven. For conventional oven, bake at 350°F for 35 to 40 minutes, until golden brown.

Yield: 6 servings

Where to Buy

Aluminum Dutch ovens in 10″ and 12″ sizes can be purchased from the following sources:

Andy & Bax
    324 S.E. Grand Avenue
    Portland, OR 97214
    (503) 234-7538
    andyandbax.com

Blackadar Boating
    (208) 940-1101
    blackadarboating.com

Cascade Outfitters
    604 E. 45th Street
    Boise, ID 83714
    (800) 223-7238
    cascadeoutfitters.com

Pacific River Supply
    3675 San Pablo Dam Road
    El Sobrante, CA 94803
    (510) 223-3675
    pacificriversupply.com

The cast-iron models often are available at hardware stores and outdoor retailers. The largest manufacturer is:

Lodge Manufacturing Company
    P.O. Box 380
    South Pittsburgh, TN 46342
    (423) 837-7181
    lodgemfg.com

Become a member of the International Dutch Oven Society by writing:

International Dutch Oven Society
    41 East 400 North, #210
    Logan, UT 84321
    idos.com

Water purifiers can be purchased through most whitewater equipment stores and catalogs. Some good sources are:

Campmor
    (201) 445-5000
    campmor.com

Eastern Mountain Sports
    all locations
    (888) 463-6367
    ems.com

L.L. Bean
    Freeport, ME 04033
    (800) 221-4221
    llbean.com

Northwest River Supplies
    P.O. Box 9186
    Moscow, ID 83843
    (800) 635-5205
    nrsweb.com

REI
    all locations
    (800) 426-4840
    rei.com

Firepans can be purchased through Northwest River Supplies and from:

Cambridge Welding
    P.O. Box 272
    Cambridge, ID 83610
    (208) 257-3589

Water filters and handwash pumps (also manufactures compact gas stoves and portable toilets):

Partner Steel
    3187 Pole Line Road
    Pocatello, ID 83701
    partnersteel.com

Index